T0114888

SECOND CHANCE

PETER DALBY

authorHOUSE®

AuthorHouse™
1663 Liberty Drive
Bloomington, IN 47403
www.authorhouse.com
Phone: 833-262-8899

© 2020 Peter Dalby. All rights reserved.

No part of this book may be reproduced, stored in a retrieval system, or transmitted by any means without the written permission of the author.

Published by AuthorHouse 10/13/2020

ISBN: 978-1-6655-0276-4 (sc)
ISBN: 978-1-6655-0277-1 (hc)
ISBN: 978-1-6655-0278-8 (e)

Print information available on the last page.

Any people depicted in stock imagery provided by Getty Images are models, and such images are being used for illustrative purposes only.
Certain stock imagery © Getty Images.

This book is printed on acid-free paper.

Because of the dynamic nature of the Internet, any web addresses or links contained in this book may have changed since publication and may no longer be valid. The views expressed in this work are solely those of the author and do not necessarily reflect the views of the publisher, and the publisher hereby disclaims any responsibility for them.

The events, names, characters, and places depicted in this story are fictitious. Any similarity to actual persons, living or deceased, or to sporting events, is purely coincidental.

I would like to thank Kailani Craine (six times Australian Senior Ladies champion and 2018 Olympian) for her very helpful advice about Australian ice skating.

1

CHARLIE WILLIAMS...GOLDEN BOY

The atmosphere became electric as the applause rose to a crescendo. With eight thousand people cheering and chanting 'CHAR-LIE, CHAR-LIE', I should have been nervous, having earlier read the newspaper headline, "*GOLDEN BOY CHARLIE GOES FOR THE HAT TRICK*", but I had trained hard for this event, and knew my routine like the back of my hand. I waited for the announcer to introduce me.

"And now, our final skater...Charles Williams!"

With a burst of energy I skated out to centre ice to take up my starting position. I breathed in steadily, filling my lungs with air, and then exhaled slowly by letting the air out through a small space between my lips. I always found this simple exercise very calming.

Almost as soon as the applause died down the first notes of my music filled the arena. I moved off, smoothly gathering speed with powerful crossovers toward my first jump. The ice felt good, and I felt 'into' it. The days of having 'Jelly' legs were long past, but then they should be. I was already a two-time British Champion, and hot favorite for a third title.

I reached back with my free leg and 'tapped' into the ice, springing up as hard as I could. Wow! That was the highest triple Lutz I'd ever done, landing right on the crescendo in the music. Tchaikovsky would have been proud! Now, it was on to some intricate footwork leading into a difficult triple toe loop-double loop combination jump. No problem here, either.

It seemed like no time at all before I reached the stage where I got my 'second wind' - that inexplicable burst of renewed energy athletes get just when they think they're exhausted - which helped me cruise through the middle section of my program into the last minute. I felt proud. So proud, because I had not let down the people who had traveled from all over England to see this championship. Each burst of applause felt like a hearty pat on the back, and I accepted it willingly as my reward for the years of sacrifice and pain that I had often endured.

Before I knew it, I was into the final element of my program, pulling my arms in close to my body to accelerate the rotation of my cross-foot spin. The world became a complete blur as I rotated faster and faster. Then, a sudden dramatic stop, and it was all over.

I was completely exhausted, but I took my customary bow and then let the energy from the standing ovation help my weary legs to carry me off toward the exit, but not before turning to give a final wave to those wonderful fans. Fans who would wait outside a stadium for two or three hours just to get a simple autograph. If only it was possible to thank each one of them individually.

As I stepped off the ice into the section known as the 'Kiss and Cry' area, my coach greeted me with a wry smile. She didn't seem overly impressed with my performance.

"You almost overdid that first jump, didn't you?" she chided. "I've told you before, things can go wrong just as easily by trying too hard as by not trying hard enough."

"Yes, I'll be more careful next time," I replied, mopping my forehead with a towel.

As usual, I could expect no emotion from my stone-faced coach. No,

Margaret Cook had seen it all before, and if you got a 'Well done' from her, it was as much as you could expect. She was a tough old 'battle axe' of a woman, but, once you got to know her, you couldn't help loving her. After all, it was the tough ones who drove you on to success.

At the ice rink where we trained, she had every one of us in tears at one time or another, but she also had that amazing ability to rip you apart, and then rebuild you to be a better skater than you were before. She was one of the 'old school' coaches who demanded respect. If you didn't say, "Good Morning, Miss Cook" when you first saw her each day, you didn't get a lesson for a week or two.

"Well," remarked Miss Cook. "I'm sure you've won, so I'm going to head back to London, now. You can have Monday off, but you'd better be back on the ice Tuesday, because you have that big International event in Budapest in two weeks time, and you don't want to lose your fitness.

"Okay, Miss Cook," I replied. "I'll be there, and...thanks for all you've done."

Cracking a slight smile as she walked away from me toward the back door of the stadium, she turned and said, "Alright, chum."

"Hey, Charlie!" a voice called out as I walked back along the corridor to the dressing room. "What a performance!" It was my mother and father, and I'd never seen them so excited. "We're so proud of you. We've never seen you skate better."

"Thanks, mum and dad," I said, getting the biggest hug I can ever remember. "I really felt confident. But you know what? Right now I just want to get changed and go back to the hotel to have something to eat. I'm starving!"

I should have realized it wasn't going to be that easy. I'd just won the British Championship, and there seemed to be a hoard of people waiting to congratulate me. One by one, they shook me by the hand, hugged me, and patted me on the back. I gratefully accepted the praise, and reminded myself that, one day, I would look back on these golden days and realize that this was the best time of my life.

Suddenly, I felt an arm around my shoulder.

"Charlie! Alastair Hodge, BBC Television. We'd like to do the interview now, if that's okay?"

"I'd be honored, Alastair. Lead the way."

He took me into the hospitality area, and we sat down.

"Cameras and audio all set?" Alistair called out.

"All set, Alastair," said a voice from behind one of the cameras. "Whenever you're ready."

"Okay, then...five, four, three, two........Good evening viewers. Alastair Hodge here, reporting from the British Ice Skating Championships. And with me is the man of the moment, Charlie Williams. Congratulations! British Champion for the third year running! How does it feel?"

"Absolutely fantastic, Alastair. I still feel like I'm in a dream, but I'm sure I'll come down to earth, soon. And I can't thank my mother and father enough for standing by me, and encouraging me through the difficult years. And my coach, Miss Cook. She's always had faith in me. And...oh, there are so many other people I want to thank. I just can't name them all."

Alastair smiled, and gave me time to compose myself. "To most of us, you made this one look easier than the two previous years. Did it seem that way to you?"

"Well...yes, and no. You see, I feel so much more experienced now, and that helped me handle the difficult elements in my program, but on the other hand, I had everything to lose, and not much to gain because I was expected to win this, so the pressure on me was enormous."

"Well, you handled it like a true champion. And now you look like being one of the favorites for the Olympic Gold Medal in Calgary in just three months time. You must be very excited."

"I certainly am, Alastair. My whole skating life has been geared toward the Olympics, and I can't tell you how proud I'm going to feel marching behind the British flag at the opening ceremony. And, if I can bring back a medal, that will be a nice bonus."

"Well, you must know that the whole of England will be rooting for you all the way."

"Wow!" I laughed. "Now *that's* what I call a fan club!"

"But, Charlie," added Alastair. "I understand that you're going to skate in an International event in Budapest in a couple of weeks. This wasn't part of your original plan, was it?"

"No, Alastair, it wasn't. I was originally going to take a short rest after the British Championships, and then train up to the European Championships and Olympics, but the Hungarian people were so gracious to me last year that I promised, in a television interview, that I would return to skate one more time. Hence, the trip to Budapest."

"Well," concluded Alastair. "It's a corny thing for me to say, but we all wish you the 'best of British luck!'"

I was still mopping the sweat from my forehead when we stood up and shook hands. The evening had been very rewarding, but also very draining, and I couldn't wait to take a shower and get changed into my street clothes.

When I got back to the hotel I headed straight for the dining room.

"Come and sit down, Charlie," said the proudest mother in the world. "We've ordered your favorite meal."

"Which is?"

"Bangers and mash, of course!"

"Oh, boy!" I exclaimed. "Bring it on."

Ever since I was a small boy, this particular dish was something I'd never tired of. It was simple, and very tasty. Nothing more, nothing less. And, on this special occasion, it just hit the spot.

It was good to relax in the company of my family and some close friends. My mother and father had always been there for me for as long as I could remember, and now, on this wonderful evening, they were beaming with pride.

My mother looked across the table at me.

"I'm so glad you made the right decision, four years ago."

"Me, too, mum. And I've never looked back since."

It had been just four years earlier that I'd wanted to quit skating. Maybe because I was disappointed that things weren't happening quickly enough. Maybe some of the excitement had gone. I don't know. But I remember clearly my mother's words that cold, foggy evening four years ago, when she sat me down for a serious talk...

"Charlie, your father and I have been thinking about your decision to quit ice skating, and, to be frank, we're very disappointed."

"I know, mum, but..."

"No, Charlie," mum interrupted. "Let me finish. Now, you know we've never insisted on you doing anything in particular. We've always let you do your own thing, but this is different. You can't just throw away something that you've worked at for the last fifteen years. What if you told everyone that you were quitting, and then, two weeks later, changed your mind? You'd look a bit silly then, wouldn't you? And I want you to think about the sacrifices your father and I have made so that you could have enough lessons. Dad's not getting any younger, you know. It's hard for him to work extra hours, but he never complains. He says it all becomes worthwhile when he sees how well you skate in your competitions."

"Oh," I murmured. "I never thought about it like that. It *is* a bit selfish of me, isn't it?"

"Well, Charlie, we'd just like you to promise us that you'll give it one more try, and persevere a bit longer. After all, what do you have to lose?"

I remember looking into her eyes, and seeing the love she had for me. And I saw how she was clutching her hands together. I didn't have to think very long.

"You're right, mum. I am being a bit hasty. I'm going to give it a really good try from now on. I really would like to be a champion."

She looked relieved as she smiled, knowing that she had given me the right advice.

How come mothers always have such good intuition?

That was just four years ago. Four years that seem to have raced by, and now it's almost the end of nineteen eighty-seven, and only three months to the Olympics. I had gone back into training in earnest, and pushed myself like I had never done before. Circumstances had turned in my favor when the champion of that time announced that he was turning professional. This had left the championship wide open, and I had as much chance to win it as anyone else. That was all I'd needed. I mastered a lot of difficult elements, and took my first title. After that confidence booster, I'd needed no encouragement to continue training hard.

My father jogged my thoughts back to the present.

"I couldn't be more proud of you, son," he said, getting up from the table. "But I'm feeling very tired now, so I'm off to bed. We have to head back to London right after breakfast tomorrow, and I don't want fall asleep at the wheel." Then he smiled, and winked his eye. "By the way, can I get your autograph now? You were mobbed like a movie star at the rink, and I'm only afraid I might have to wait in line!"

"I know," I laughed. "I never thought I'd get out of there. No wonder Miss Cook wanted to make a quick exit."

2

A FACE ACROSS A CROWDED ROOM

~⁓○⁓~

The days leading up to my trip to Budapest went by quickly. Probably because I had so many things to attend to, not to mention my daily training regime. This now included off-ice exercises, and trips to my local gym for strength training. Gone were the days when you could just treat this sport as a pastime. Everyone meant business now, and if you snooze, you lose.

The last week of my training became quite intense.

"Charlie! If you don't check the turn into that jump, you'll never have control of your take-off edge," yelled Miss Cook.

"Yes, okay. I think I'm putting too much energy into the turn. I'll try another one, and be a bit more subtle."

I went around the rink again and set up the jump.

"Now," shouted Miss Cook. "Check.....UP.....and OUT! That's much better."

That's what I liked about Miss Cook. She noticed every detail. You *knew* she was totally focused on her work, and absolutely lived for it.

"Hey, Charlie," a voice behind me whispered. "Cathy and Louise are all set to go to the cinema with us this weekend. Are you on?"

It was Don Hastings, another Miss Cook product. He had spent most of the morning chatting up the two most beautiful girls training at the rink.

Don was a good friend, but just didn't take anything too seriously. Some people joked that he only came into the rink to get out of the rain. He was a happy-go-lucky sort who came from a well-to-do family, and treated life like there was no tomorrow. Girls and fast cars were uppermost in his mind, with ice skating ranking about fourth or fifth on his list of priorities.

"Get out of here, Don. I'm in a lesson."

"Okay. I'll talk to you in the locker room."

Don went off the ice, and left me trying to work on a triple jump with Cathy and Louise now on my mind. Thanks, Don.

At the end of the morning's training I went back into the locker room and sat down beside him.

"Oooh...that feels good," I sighed, as I eased my skates off my aching feet.

"Come on, Charlie, put your shoes on. I've just got enough time to have a couple of pints with you 'round at the 'Black Swan', before I head home."

"No way, I'm afraid, Don. I leave for Budapest in a few days, and I've got to stay in peak shape. But I'll have a pint with you when I come back."

"Alright, party-pooper," he said, patting me on the back. "At least I know you've got a genuine reason."

"But the cinema this weekend sounds great, Don. I haven't seen a movie in months, and, besides, I couldn't stand the thought of you having Cathy and Louise all to yourself."

The weekend came and went, and all too soon I was on my way out to Heathrow airport for my flight to Budapest.

"Slow down, dad," I said. "My flight doesn't leave for another two hours."

"I just want to make sure we're not going to be late," he replied.

"Now, have you got everything, Charlie?" said mum, concerned as usual.

"Yes, mum," I replied. "I'll be back again in a few days, so I didn't need to pack a whole lot of stuff."

Thirty minutes later, I was unloading my bags out of the car, helped by my ever-worrying mother.

"Watch out for that spicy food, Charlie." she went on. "I've heard that they have Goulash for breakfast."

"Oh, mum! Where did you hear that?"

"Well, see if you can bring me back a recipe for it. We'll cook up some for the neighbors."

Eventually dad managed to get a word in. "Okay. Now, have you got everything, son?"

"Yes, thanks, Dad. I'm all set."

He put his arm around my shoulders, and gave me a gentle mock punch on the chin.

"We're proud of you, son. You just go and skate your heart out, and let 'em see what you're made of."

"I will, dad. You'll see."

I turned around to see my mother pulling out her handkerchief. "Oh, mum! What are those tears for? Anyone would think I was going away for six months."

"Oh, you know how I am, Charlie. I always feel a bit emotional any time you go away."

I put my arms around her, and gave her a big hug. "You know something? You're the best mum I've ever had!"

"Oh, Charlie. Sometimes you're so silly."

"Okay. 'Bye mum and dad. Take care."

I picked up my bags and went into the terminal to find the rest of the team.

The flight to Budapest is only about two and a half hours from London, but it gave me the chance to catch up on a little sleep.

The take-off was as smooth as silk, and after the seat belt sign had been turned off, I reclined my seat, closed my eyes, and began to think back to how all this started. It made me smile, because I thought back to the unlikely chain of events that caused me to be sitting here at this moment. Here I was, jetting off to yet another International competition, and all because of a flat tire, many years ago. A small inconvenience at the time, but one that was to change my life.

Many people, at some time in their lives, come to a fork in the road, and have to make a decision on which way their lives will go, but my direction in life was decided for me by something as simple as a flat tire. The signpost pointed only one way.

It all happened one sunny Sunday afternoon about twelve years before, when my parents decided that we would all try horse riding at a riding school in Surrey. About a mile from our destination, dad felt that something was wrong with the car, and pulled over to the side of the road. When he got out he discovered that we had a flat tire, and immediately set about changing it. This mishap cost us about thirty minutes, and by the time we arrived at the riding school the horses and riders were already walking out of the yard, headed by a very stern-looking riding master. Dad caught up with him and tried to explain about our flat tire, but was greeted with a very arrogant reply.

"I don't care about your excuses. You were supposed to be here at two o'clock, and it's now two thirty, so I can't hang around here talking all day. You're holding up the ride." And with that, he trotted off.

Dad was livid!

"What a pompous twit!" he fumed. "We're not going to take lessons in this place. We'll have a drive around, and find somewhere else."

And so we did. We found a much friendlier place, and started riding each Sunday afternoon.

A couple of years later, I became friendly with some other riders of my age, and we hung out a lot together. One day, one of them said,

"Hey, there's a new ice rink that's opened not far from here. Why don't we all go skating together?"

"That sounds like a good idea," I replied. "I skated a little bit when I was about ten, so it would be fun to try it again." The others thought it was a great idea, too, and a few days later we were on the ice, slipping, sliding, and having a barrel of laughs.

When I told my parents about it, they decided that they, too, would like to try, so, a few days later, off we went.

On the ice, I just wanted to tear around like a maniac, but they eventually convinced me that we should all take some lessons. Well, as is so often the case, one thing led to another, and before I knew it I found myself getting more and more involved in the intense world of competitive ice skating. That was all several years ago.

A smile came across my face, as I wondered what other adventures fate had in store for me.

A hand shook my shoulder. "Wake up Charlie, we're here," said our team leader.

"Oh...I didn't even feel the plane landing."

As soon as we got off the plane, we found that everything was nicely organized, and, once outside the airport, a luxurious bus quickly sped us to our hotel.

That evening, we all attended the welcoming reception and draw party at the elegant Town Hall. The President of the Hungarian Skating Association rose to his feet.

"Mr. Mayor, Lady Mayoress, honored officials of the I.S.U.(International Skating Union), ladies and gentlemen, and, last but not least, skaters. On behalf of the Hungarian Skating Federation, I welcome you to 'Skate Budapest'. We hope you will enjoy our beautiful city, and we know that you will participate in our competition with the spirit of good sportsmanship that you are known for. I will now ask my colleagues to proceed with the draw for the starting order."

The officials set up a huge numbered board, and then systematically read out each name on the list of entries.

"Vladimir Shiznovski?"

"Here!"

"Abilla Bongoragamon?"

"Yes!"

"Nikos Papakopalopolis?"

"Here!"

"George Smith?"

"Here!"

And so it went on. For the next thirty minutes, one skater after another went up and reached into the velvet bag that held all the numbered balls. Some smiled, and some frowned, but once this was over, we could get down to the best part of the evening. Food! Our hosts had laid on a sumptuous international buffet, and we wasted no time in filling our plates.

"Okay, boys and girls," said out team leader, George Barton, trying to make himself heard above all the noise. "Enjoy yourselves, be good ambassadors, and we'll meet outside the front door at nine to get the bus back to the hotel."

Everyone was standing in groups, elbow to elbow, and I was just about to make polite conversation with a total stranger, when I glanced across to the other side of this very crowded hall. Through a sea of faces, I saw an incredibly beautiful girl, who happened to look my way at the same time.

"Oh, excuse me," I said to my bewildered stranger. "I need to get some water."

Holding my plate over my head, I squeezed my way passed at least fifty closely-grouped people, and eventually came face to face with her.

"Hello," I said, as cheerfully as I could.

"Hello," she replied shyly.

"I haven't seen you before. What country do you represent?"

"U.S.A. This is my first International event, and I'm a little nervous."

"Oh, I'll bet you'll skate beautifully."

I smiled stupidly at her for a few seconds, and then realized I hadn't introduced myself.

"Oh...my name's Charlie."

"Yes, I already know that. I've seen your picture in lots of skating magazines. My name's Cindy."

"It's really nice to meet you, Cindy. By the way, have you had any food yet?"

"No. I was just going to get some."

"In that case, I'll come along and help you select the most nutritious items, so that you'll be the healthiest skater in the event!"

She laughed. "That would be very nice of you. From now on, you're my nutritional advisor."

Well, I thought, it's a start.

We made our way over to the buffet, and started filling our plates.

"You know, Cindy, my skating has taken me all over Europe and behind the Iron Curtain, but I've never been to America."

"Oh, you don't know what you're missing. There's so much to see. They say you can see the whole world in the U.S.A. Mind you, it's such a big country, I have to admit I've only seen a small part of it, myself."

We chatted on about everything and anything for the next hour or so, until it was time for me to go back to the hotel.

"Maybe I'll see you tomorrow, Cindy...at the practice session?"

"Okay," she smiled. "I'll watch out for you. 'Bye."

On the bus ride back to the hotel, our team leader glanced across at me.

"You're looking pretty pleased with yourself, Charlie."

I smiled back contentedly. "Yes, it's been a great evening."

For the next two days, I figured out all sorts of ways to be near Cindy, like staying to watch her on a practice session that followed mine. That way, I made sure I'd ride back on the same bus with her to the hotel.

"Here, let me take your skate bag," I said, as we climbed onto the bus the next day.

"Thanks, Charlie, That's very nice of you."

"You know, I feel I've know you for much longer than two days."

"I know. Doesn't it seem like much longer? But I've really enjoyed talking to you."

"Well, I was thinking...even though I can't come to America right now, we could write to each other...if that's okay?"

"Of course it is! That would be nice. And maybe, one day soon, you'll be able to come over and see it."

On the final day of practice, there was a large crowd of people waiting for autographs as we came out of the rink to get on the bus. Cindy and I put down our skate bags and were only too happy to oblige these dedicated skating fans.

"Koszonom!" said an older gentleman, as I handed him back his book.

"Pardon?" I replied.

"Is Hungarian for 'Thank you!'"

"Oh! Then...Koszonom to you, too! It's very nice of you to wait for us."

After we'd signed a few more books, a voice called out from inside the bus.

"The bus is going, Charlie. Hurry up!"

"That's okay. You go on back. I'm going to walk back through the city." I turned to Cindy. "You know what? The hotel's not far away. Would you like to walk back with me, and see a little of Budapest? It's such a beautiful city, and you never know if you'll ever get another chance to see it."

Cindy smiled.

"That sounds like a great idea. Let's go."

We waved as the bus pulled away, and threw our skate bags over our shoulders. It was a beautiful day, and I was looking forward to seeing something of this fairytale city, so beautifully situated on the River Danube.

"You know, Cindy, so often we skaters never have the time to explore these exciting new places, as we are either eating or sleeping at the hotel, practicing or competing at the ice rink, or going back and forth on the bus. At a lot of competitions the order of the day is: Hotel, bus, ice rink, bus, hotel. And that's often repeated at least once more the same day."

We strolled along for about ten minutes before I realized we were lost.

"Excuse me," I called out to a man who happened to be leaning on the balcony of his house. "Er...where is Castle Hill...for the Castle? How do we get there?"

Fortunately, he seemed to understand English.

"You must cross the Szechenyi Chain Bridge. You see it? Over there in the distance?"

"Oh, yes. Thanks!" I said, giving him an appreciative wave.

He took his pipe out of his mouth, nodded, and smiled.

We walked along the street in the direction of the bridge, but, just ahead of us, I happened to notice a group of children crossing the street, heading for the *'Great Circus'*. One little girl, who was lagging behind, tried to catch up, but the traffic light had already turned to red. Sometimes, kids of that age just don't see these things, and she ran straight out into the road to try to catch up with her friends.

"HEY...LITTLE GIRL!" I yelled. "STOP! LOOK OUT!"

A truck was hurtling toward her, but she couldn't understand what I was yelling.

"LOOK OUT! LOOK OUT!"

"Oh, my God!" I thought.

I don't know what made me do it, but I sprinted into the middle of the street toward her. She couldn't see the horrific scene unfolding, but I could see the driver wasn't going to be able to stop in time. I dived at her, grabbed her arm, and flung her further across the road. She screamed.

"Oh, NO!" I yelled, as the truck bore down on me. People started screaming. There was a terrible squealing of brakes, and the driver tried hard to swerve around me, but it was too late. As I tried to scramble to my feet, the truck went over my right ankle. Then, everything went blank...

3

Life Takes A Cruel Turn

"Mr. Williams?...Mr. Williams?" a voice seemed to be saying in the distance.

My eyelids felt heavy, but I managed to half open them.

"Ooh," I groaned. "Water...water." I tried to swallow, but my mouth felt like a parched desert. "Water...please."

"Nurse, you may give him some water." said a voice in the background.

I sipped the water, and then took a deep breath, and sighed.

"Where am I?"

"In a Budapest hospital," the voice said, calmly. "You've had a bad accident." Then he paused. "Do you remember?"

"Er...no. Oh...wait a minute. Yes, the truck...now I remember." I opened my eyes a little more, and saw a group of people standing around the bed. Then it all came flooding back to me.

"The little girl! Is she okay?"

"Yes, you probably saved her life. Her parents don't know how to thank you. They said they will be forever grateful to you."

"Oh...well...I wasn't trying to be a hero, or anything like that. Something made me do it. I couldn't help myself."

The voice in the background turned out be Dr. Szabo, head of the orthopedic department.

"Yours was an act of pure instinct. A sudden impulse to save a fellow human being from disaster. In situations like this, there is no time to think. We just react."

"What happens next, Doctor?"

"Well, we're going to take some more X-rays, and then wait until the swelling goes down before we put you in a cast. Then, you'll be able to travel home and see a specialist in London."

"Thank you....Oh my God! Do my parents know what's happened? And our Team Leader? I have to go and withdraw from the competition!"

I tried to sit up to get out of bed, but I could hardly move my leg.

"Mr. Williams. Please remain calm. You cannot get out of bed, yet, but everything has been taken care of. Your parents are waiting for you to telephone them, and your team leader has been informed."

"Oh...I'm sorry. I'm just...well, this is all so sudden. Is this really happening?"

"Yes. I'm afraid so." said a nurse.

I laid my head back on the pillow and tried to gather my thoughts. Let me see, now. I've had, what seems to be, a fairly bad accident, and I'm definitely out of *this* competition. Okay. Keep calm. I just need to get back to England, and start rehabilitation to get ready for the European Championships, and the Olympics. I can make it. I can be ready in time. I *have* to think positive thoughts.

Just then, I heard a familiar voice outside my room.

"Is he allowed visitors?"

"Cindy! Please let her in, nurse."

Cindy rushed into the room, and into my open arms.

"Oh, Charlie," she sobbed. "I've been so worried about you."

"There, there. Calm down." I held her close to me, and her hair felt so good as it flopped across my face. I hugged her, and whispered in her ear,

"You just don't know how pleased I am to see you."

"Oh, I'm just so glad you're okay, Charlie."

"I'm going to be fine, so please try not to worry. I don't want anything to upset your chances in the competition."

She sighed. "Well, I feel a lot better now that I've seen you. I skate tomorrow."

She lifted up her head, and looked at me. Her eyes were a little puffy, but she managed to crack a smile, and that was better than any tonic the hospital could have given me.

"Now, Cindy. Tomorrow, I want you to go out and skate like you haven't a care in the world. I'll be thinking of you, and willing you all my strength. Will you do that?"

"Oh, you bet I will! I'm going to skate this one for you. You'll be proud of me."

"That's my girl!"

Just then, the nurse entered the room.

"I am sorry, but you will have to leave now," she said curtly. "I have to give Mr. Williams his medication, and he also needs to rest."

"I think you'd better go, Cindy, while the going's good. But, good luck tomorrow. You'll be a sensation."

"Okay, Charlie. I feel a lot better, now."

I swallowed a couple of pills, laid my head back on the pillow, and drifted off to sleep with a contented smile on my face.

The next day, time seemed to stand still. The hours go by slowly enough when you're in hospital, but this was the longest day I could remember. I couldn't wait to find out what had happened at the skating competition, but there was nothing I could do, but wait. The ladies competition was taking place between two o'clock and five, and it was now five-thirty. That meant the results should be known by now, and, hopefully, she'll be on her way over to see me.

Another hour went by.

"Mr. Williams," the nurse said. "Please eat your dinner."

"Oh...I'm not that hungry right now"

"Are you not feeling well?"

"No, it's not that. It's...er...well, nothing."

"Mr. Williams, I'm sure she'll be here soon. Now, please try to eat."

"Okay. Thank you, nurse."

I picked up my fork, and started picking away at my dinner. At least, it did help pass away the time.

Just as I finished, I saw a hand appear around the door frame, holding a medal dangling on a ribbon.

"Yoohoo!"

My spirits rose in less than a second.

"Cindy! You got a medal?"

"Better than that." she replied, sticking her head around the door, smiling. "I got a gold medal!"

"Whoopee!" I yelled out. "Come over here, and let me give you a big hug."

"Oh, my God, Charlie, I thought of you just before the warm-up, and it made me feel so strong. I was never going to admit this to anyone, but I've always been a bit scared of my double axel, but when I was approaching it in my program I just thought of your courage, and it made me jump higher than ever. I didn't have a moment's hesitation. You inspired me to go for it."

"Oh, Cindy, I'm so proud of you! I didn't think anything could make me feel good after what's happened, but I feel as good as if I'd won the medal myself."

"Charlie, my day has been so wonderful, but what about you, now? Have they told you yet when you can go home?"

"Well, I think they're going to be giving me a final check-up tomorrow, and then, all being well, I can leave the next day."

"Oh, that's great news! And I'm going to write a letter to you as soon as I get home."

"I'll be sitting by the front door every day, waiting for it to drop into our letterbox."

Two days later, the time came for me to bid farewell to my doctors and nurses. I couldn't thank them enough. I would never forget how they helped me through a very difficult time. I think they deliberately kept my thoughts occupied, so that I wouldn't have too much time to reflect on what had happened to me.

It turned out, though, that there was one unexpected advantage to having a huge plaster cast on my leg. Because I needed more room, I got to sit in the first-class section of the plane for my flight back to London!

4

THE PAINFUL TRUTH

As I came out of the baggage claim area at Heathrow, I was met by a barrage of reporters and photographers. I wasn't expecting this but, obviously, news gets around. I leaned on my crutches and did the best I could to put on a brave smile. One by one, the sports reporters fired one question after another at me.

"Charlie, how long do you think you'll need to recover?"

"Do you think you'll be okay for the Olympics?"

"How bad is the injury?"

Another reporter put his hand on my shoulder and said,

"Hey, Charlie. When we said, 'Break a leg', we didn't mean it literally!" That made everyone laugh, including myself.

After they'd asked all their questions, and taken their photographs, they gradually dispersed, and there, waiting patiently behind them, were my mother and father. Mum came up to me and gave me a big hug.

"Welcome home, Charlie. It's not the way we thought we'd be welcoming you, but it's lovely to see you home again safe and sound. Well, almost sound."

"Hello mum and dad. Oh, dear. It's been quite an adventure. Did the team leader tell you all about it?"

"Yes, son." replied my father. "He kept us well informed. So we'll just have to keep our fingers crossed, and hope for the best. That was a very brave thing you did, and I'm proud of you. If you'd gone back to the hotel on the bus, that little girl might not be alive today. You're quite the hero in our neighborhood."

"Oh, I don't want to be a hero. Anybody else would have done the same thing."

"Well then. Let's get in the car, and go home."

As we walked out to the parking area, my mother said,

"Now don't you worry. Stan Collins called from the skating association and said they've arranged for you to see the best specialist in Harley Street. He'll have you up and skating in no time."

"Oh, I'm sure it's going to heal up just beautifully." I replied."

The next day, I found myself at an orthopedic surgeons office in Harley Street. My mother knocked on the door.

"Oh, come in, Charlie. I'm Doctor Caldwell. And you must be Mrs. Williams. It's very nice to meet you."

He shook our hands and smiled, but I could sense he was uneasy about something.

"Do come in and sit down."

We made ourselves comfortable and waited to hear what he had to say.

"Let me show you these X-rays so you can understand the situation."

He clipped them onto a screen, and switched on the light. I got up to have a closer look.

"Now, you see that grey area there? Well, that's the part of the bone that's been crushed. Right by the joint. Now, It'll heal to a certain extent, but..."

He turned away from me, and sighed. I realized it was time to put on a brave face.

"So...what's the verdict, Doc? Am I going to be able to skate again? Or even walk?"

"Oh, you'll walk again alright, Charlie," said Dr. Caldwell. "That won't be a problem. But...well...I'm sorry to have to be the one to break this to you, but this ankle of yours is so badly damaged, it will never stand up to the stresses of competitive ice skating again."

He leaned on his desk, and paused.

"I'm afraid it's the end of the line for you as a competitor, and I'm so, so sorry."

I felt devastated. Was he telling me that at the relatively tender age of twenty-two, I was finished? Wait a minute, I thought, I can't quite get a handle on this.

I sat down by his desk and tried to come to terms with what he had just told me.

"I'm so used to training every day, and now that's *over*?"

"I'm afraid so, Charlie."

"Oh, my God. I've got so used to my daily routine, I never thought it would ever end."

"I know, Charlie."

He paused, and then went on.

"Well...you're going to have to be very understanding now, and realize that everything has to come to an end at some time, although it *is* so tragic that your career has been cut short by such a freak accident. You're going to have to be brave, and find the strength to take a different direction in your life. There are plenty of new challenges out there, Charlie, and I know you'll meet them with success."

"Yes...er...well..."

I couldn't find any words. I knew Doctor Caldwell was trying to soften the blow as much as possible, but there was no hiding from the impact of the news.

I didn't feel sorrow, or grief. In fact I didn't really feel anything. I just felt numb.

My mother drove me home in almost total silence. I just stared out of the window at the blur of traffic going in the opposite direction. Then, it all began to come home to me, and I buried my face in my hands.

"Oh, Charlie," said my mother. "You're going to have me crying, too, in a minute. And I have to drive us home. You poor, poor thing. You just let it all out."

"Thanks, mum. I...I just don't know what I'd do without you and dad."

"Now don't you worry. But I don't know how your father's going to take this when he gets home. I think he was expecting *good* news. Anyway, you know what they say, every cloud has a silver lining, so we'll have to see what the future holds."

That evening, after I'd finished my dinner, I just had one thought on my mind that gave me something to live for.

"Mum? Do you have some writing paper, and a pen? I want to write to Cindy."

"Yes, Charlie. I'll go and get you some."

She brought in some writing paper and put it on the table. I closed my eyes, and tried to come up with some opening words. Then I picked up my pen and started writing.

> *Dear Cindy,*
>
> *How are you? That's how most people start a letter, isn't it? Well, I hope you're really well and in great spirits after your big win in Budapest. I couldn't be happier for you, and our friendship is the only thing that's keeping me going.*
>
> *I felt on top of the world being British champion, like I was somebody, but now I feel like my whole world has fallen apart. You see, the bad news is that my skating days are over. The injury to my ankle was worse than I thought, and the doctor said it would never stand up to the strain of competitive skating. So that's it.*
>
> *A few days ago I felt important, but now I feel like I'm a nobody, and I don't have any confidence in myself any more. I hope I can see you again, one day. Please write back to me if you can. You're very special.*
>
> *Love, Charlie.*

The days went by, and I was beginning to think that meeting Cindy had just been a dream, but then, one morning, my mother came into my bedroom with a silly smile on her face. "Charlie. There's a letter here with an American stamp on it. I wonder who that could be from?"

"Oh, my God! Give it to me, quickly!"

I tore open the letter, and read its contents.

> *Dear Charlie,*
>
> *I was so excited to get your letter. I read it over and over again, and now (please don't laugh) I put it under my pillow when I go to bed each night. Is that silly?*
>
> *Oh, Charlie, I feel so sorry for you. I know there are no words that can make you feel better, but please know that I think about you every day, and pray that a miracle will happen so you'll be able to skate again. This is the 1980's, and they've made incredible progress with surgical techniques. You never know, they might even be able to make you stronger than you were before. Anyway, keep your chin up, and believe!*
>
> *I'm so glad we met. You've given me such confidence, and I know I can achieve more and more. I'm counting the days until we meet again.*
>
> *Take good care of yourself. I'll be checking the mailbox every day for your next letter.*
>
> *Love, Cindy*

My first thought was that I wanted to put *her* letter under *my* pillow, but on second thoughts that didn't seem a very manly thing to do. I'd settle for keeping it in a drawer along with, hopefully, many more of her letters.

A few days later I had a phone call from Steve Collins at the National Skating Association.

"Charlie. How are you?"

"Not too bad, thanks, Mr. Collins. How are you?"

"I'm doing fine, thanks, Charlie, but I'll get straight to the point.

Now, you know Jimmy Donovan, the Junior champion? He's improving fast, and we're really excited about him as a future Olympic prospect..."

"I know," I interrupted. "In a year or two I'd have been very worried about him, myself."

"Well, that's the point, you see," continued Mr. Collins. "We're looking for someone who can teach him the technique for all these new elements that are essential for success, and, as you know, Madge Livingstone has coached him since he was a little nipper. Now, we all like Madge, and she's a very good coach, but even *she* has confided to us that she's not sure if she's going to be able to take him to the higher levels. She's never been to any International events, and is quite unknown abroad. To tell you the truth, Charlie, she's already told us that you'd have her blessing to take over Jimmy's training if you'd like to. So, there you are. You still have the chance to do something really worthwhile."

"Wow! That does sound like a great opportunity for me."

"Well, Charlie. Think it over for a couple of days, and then we'll talk again."

It didn't take me more than a few minutes to make up my mind. Not only was it a great opportunity, but what else was I going to do with my life? Fate was offering me second chance to do something worthwhile, in a sport that I loved, and I would have been a fool not to grab it with both hands.

I called him right back again.

"Mr. Collins? I don't even have to think about it. I'll take the job. It's just way too good to pass up. And I can assure you, I'm going to do *anything* I have to, to be a successful coach."

That evening, I thought it would only be right to give Madge a call, so I picked up the phone and dialed her number.

"Melford 3427."

"Hello, is that Madge Livingstone?"

"Yes. Is that Charlie?"

"Yes, Madge. It's me. I wanted to call you to chat about Jimmy."

"Certainly, Charlie. I'm glad you've called."

"But, first of all," I said, "I want to thank you for recommending me. It's very unselfish of you, and I can't tell you how grateful I am. You're giving me a great start to what I hope will be a successful coaching career."

"Not at all, Charlie. I was only too glad to put your name forward, and it seems like the timing couldn't be better for both of us. You see, I come from an era when skaters were just doing double jumps, and although I've moved with the times and learned how to teach triple jumps, I'm not really comfortable with the way that skating is advancing so quickly. And I'd hate to hold Jimmy back from what looks like being a very promising career. So I'm very happy he'll be in your capable hands, and I wish you both the very best of luck."

"Well, thank you, Madge. You know I'll do my best. And I hope it's alright to call you 'Madge'? I remember when I was eight years old having some lessons with you, and I had to call you Mrs. Livingstone. You would have given me a clip 'round the ear if I'd called you 'Madge' back then!"

"No, that's fine, Charlie." she replied, laughing. "We're both fellow coaches now, even though I do have a few years on you."

"Well, Madge, I'm not just saying this, but you haven't changed a bit since I first saw you."

"Oh, well you know what they say. An ice rink is very much like a meat locker, so with all the hours we spend in them, it stands to reason that we keep for a long time!"

"Ha ha! You always did have a great sense of humor, Madge, but how long have you been coaching?"

"It'll be fifty years this November. Can you believe it? And the scary thing is that the time seems to have flown by. And, of course, when I was competing the school figures were the main part of the competition. We used to spend three hours a day practicing them on beautiful ice that was like a sheet of glass. Most of the coaches back then were real 'old school' types, and as grumpy as hell. But there was discipline and respect, which really wasn't a bad thing."

It was great listening to Madge relating how things were in the 'old days'. And she certainly had the respect of all her students. She, and my coach, Miss Cook, had pretty much been the backbone of British figure skating.

"So, is there anything I should know about Jimmy? I mean, is he a hard worker? Or sensitive? Or does he have any bad habits?"

Madge thought for a moment, and then said,

"No, he doesn't have any bad habits, but he is a bit of a worrier. His father is very strict with him, and expects him to be a winner every time. I've tried to take the pressure off him by praising him whenever possible, and giving him as much encouragement as I can, but he's still very uptight and doesn't find it easy to relax.

"Okay. Thanks, Madge. That will help me to understand him. I'll keep in touch with you and let you know how he's doing."

5

My Second Chance!

~~~⟨⟩~~~

The following Monday morning I stood by the ice at Melford Ice Rink, ready to start my new career. Having a bit of a name in skating was a real plus, and word had got around that I was going to be working there.

Within a few days I was teaching quite a few private lessons, and it felt good to be earning my own money. Apart from the money, though, I found that teaching has it's own rewards. It gave me a sense of pride to see the excitement and joy in a child's face after seeing them master even a simple jump. And to think that I was getting paid for this...well, I *almost* felt guilty.

At the end of my first week, I counted all the money I'd earned, and decided to repay some of the kindness my parents had showered on me over the years. They had skimped on so many things, and saved every pound so that I could have the lessons I needed, and one of the things my mother always dreamed of was a dishwashing machine. Every evening, while she was washing the dishes after dinner, she would say how luxurious it would be to sit down and put her feet up, while a machine did the work for her. Well, now, I was in a position to make her dream come true.

Two days later, I had just finished breakfast and was just about to leave for the rink when there was a knock at the door.

"I wonder who that can be?" said my mother. "I'm not expecting anyone this morning."

"Well," I said, "There's only way to find out."

She opened the door.

"Good morning, ma'am." Are you Mrs. Williams?"

"Yes, that's me. What can I do for you?"

"We're from Bellingham's, and we have a delivery for you."

"Really? What can that be?"

"A nice shiny new dishwasher, ma'am. Didn't you know about it?"

Mum turned to me, with her mouth hanging open.

"Charlie. Do you know anything about this?"

"I certainly do, mum. And it's the least you deserve."

"Oh, Charlie." mum gasped. "What a son you are! But you can't go spending your hard-earned money on me like this."

"Mum, I wish I could buy you a new house, too, to put it in, but don't you think you'd better let the men bring it in? They're waiting."

"Oh, I am sorry." she said, turning back to the men. "If you'd like to come in, gentlemen, I'll show you where the kitchen is."

Mother, completely nonplussed, led them into the kitchen.

"Well, I suppose you could put it over there." she said, pointing to a space near the sink.

"Yes, I think that will do very nicely," said the man. "So if you'll just give us a couple of hours, we'll have it all fixed up, and ready to operate."

As the men started to bring in the dishwasher, I went over to my mother and gave her a big hug.

"Thank you...thank you, Charlie. It's such a thoughtful gift."

The tears were streaming down her cheeks, and I knew she was feeling like a kid at Christmas-time.

"I really do have to get to the rink, now, mum, so I'll see you later."

"Okay, Charlie. And thanks again. Ooh! I'm so excited!"

I really did have to be at the rink on time this particular morning, because this is the first day I start teaching Jimmy Donovan.

Jimmy, to his credit, was there right on time.

"I'm really looking forward to taking lessons from you, Charlie." Jimmy said, holding out his hand. "But, I don't know. Should I call you *Mr.* Williams, now?"

"No," I laughed. "But just make sure you show a little respect!"

"Okay," agreed Jimmy. "I will."

I then went over a rough outline of how I wanted him to train over the next few weeks. Being the Junior Men's champion, he would be going to a couple of Junior International competitions in the not-too-distant future, so we didn't have all that long to work on technique, and making sure his freestyle program had all the necessary elements.

Jimmy really was quite talented, and coaching him was the next best thing to actually being out there on the ice, myself.

After working with him for a couple of weeks, I couldn't wait to get home and write to Cindy, to tell her how excited I was to have such a promising pupil.

> *Dear Cindy,*
>
> *I don't know where to begin! I miss you so much, and I would give anything for you to be with me right now. But, at least I have that to look forward to in the future.*
>
> *I'm really excited that I'm now the coach of our Junior champion, Jimmy Donovan. He's good! He really would have been serious competition for me in a year or two. So it may be a blessing in disguise that I've started coaching now, because I might have missed this opportunity later on. But I have to admit, there isn't a day that goes by that I don't want to go out there and peel off a big jump, but, I guess you could say my wings are clipped, now.*
>
> *I thank God that I have you in my life, and your support. I wouldn't know what to do with myself without that. With you, the future holds some promise for me. After I've earned some more money this year, I want to*

> *fly over to the U.S.A. and see you again, and maybe meet*
> *your parents. I hope they'll like me!*
> *Well, please take good care of yourself, and I'll write*
> *again soon.*
>
> *Love,*
> *Charlie*

The following day, I couldn't help noticing a marked difference in Jimmy's energy level. I knew, as he grew older, that he would strengthen naturally, but he suddenly seemed to be skating with more vigor than ever.

"Jimmy! I really like the new man I see before me. Where did all this 'pep' come from?"

"Er...well...I'm on a high-energy diet, and I'm also taking multi vitamins and eating lots of vegetables, y'know."

"Well, whatever it is you're doing, keep up the good work."

When I got home that evening, I'd hardly got in the door when the 'phone rang.

"Hello?"

"Charlie? It's Steve Collins."

"Oh, hello Mr. Collins. What can I do for you?"

"Well, Charlie, things are happening quickly. Jimmy has been selected for the Junior International in Vienna in about five weeks, so you'll be off to your first competition as a coach. What do you think of that?"

"Wow, I'm excited! We've been working hard, so he'll be ready. I think you'll like what I've done to his program. He's got about as much technical difficulty as he can handle, but he's coping very well. I just can't believe how powerfully he's skating. He's like a different person."

"Okay then Charlie. Make sure both of your passports are in order, and I'll get back to you as soon as we have all the details."

I put down the phone, and started to think about all the things I would need for the trip.

The day before we left for Vienna, another letter came from Cindy.

Dear Charlie,

First of all, I want to tell you that I miss you more than ever! I'm so glad you have your coaching job, but even if you didn't, I wouldn't care. Whatever you do is fine with me. You don't have to be a champion for me to care about you. It's Charlie Williams I like, not the champion you became. It will take you a long time to get over the bitter disappointment of never being able to compete again, but I know you'll cope with it, and make the best of your second chance in life.

I love you,
Cindy

I must have read that letter ten times before I put it in my suitcase. I decided that it was going to be my good luck charm, and would go with me to every competition.

The flight to Vienna was uneventful, and we arrived in plenty of time to put in some practice that evening. As soon as I walked into the rink, I heard a familiar voice behind me.

"Charlie Williams! Mein God, how are you?"

I turned to see the familiar face of Gunther Schnabel, West Germany's top coach. He came up to me and gave me a huge bear hug.

"Hello, Herr Schnabel. I'm okay, I think. But it's good to see you again."

"We are all so sorry about what happened to you." he said. "Are you managing alright? I hear you are now a coach."

"Yes, that's right. And now I'm going to give you a run for your money!"

"Well, I certainly hope you do. You deserve to have lots of success as a coach, and I give you my very best wishes."

"Thank you, Herr Schnabel. Coming from you, that's very encouraging."

"So, I'll see you tomorrow at the competition, Charlie."

"Yes, see you then."

Jimmy's practice session went very well, and I was quietly confident of having a good start to my coaching career. It would look good for me back home if I could get Jimmy to produce his best, but I didn't want to push him too hard because he seemed a little fragile.

We went back to the hotel, had a nice relaxing dinner with the rest of the team, and then got an early night in readiness for the big day.

The next morning, after a short practice session and a light lunch, we boarded the bus to go back to the rink.

"Jimmy, when we get to the rink I have to go and get my accreditation, but I want you to start going over your stretch exercises outside the dressing room. That way, I'll know where to find you."

"Okay, Charlie. I'll do that."

Once I'd received my accreditation I went straight down to the dressing room to see how Jimmy was warming up.

"Are you ready, Jimmy?"

"Er...yes. I'd better put on my skates, now."

With that, he disappeared into the dressing room in a hurry.

It wasn't long before it was show time, and Jimmy's group took the ice for their warm-up.

The warm-up went very well, with Jimmy landing all his jumps, and spinning faster than I'd ever seen him. As he came off the ice, I handed him his water bottle.

"Here, Jimmy. Just take a few sips, because you're the next to skate after this guy."

Jimmy eagerly drank some water, and then wiped his face with a towel. His breathing rate was fast, but I put this down to him being excited at the prospect of competing.

What worried me, though, was that I'd seen Jimmy at competitions before, but I'd never seen him this wound up. I know it was an International event, but he'd had lots of experience skating before a crowd, and shouldn't have been in such a state.

"Okay, Jimmy." I said. We've been over what you need to concentrate on in your program, so now it's just a matter of performing it well. You get out there and show them who's best."

It was as though he hadn't heard a word I said. When his turn came, he leapt out onto the ice and went over to his starting position.

The music started, and he immediately built up tremendous speed for his first jump, a double axel. He sprang high into the air, and landed it perfectly. I just prayed that he would pace himself, and not use up all his energy too soon. Then, far from getting more tired as he continued through the program, he started rushing things, and actually got ahead of his music. He was skating like a man possessed. His jumps started to get erratic, he failed to center his spins, and ended up looking very ragged. Overall, it wasn't really a bad performance, but it could have been so much better.

He came off the ice, and nearly collapsed into my arms.

"Jimmy! Are you alright?" I said, as he staggered over to the 'Kiss and Cry' area.

"Yes. I'll be okay in a minute." he replied, grabbing a towel to mop the sweat off his face.

"Well, try to calm down while we wait for your marks to come up."

We watched anxiously as each judge's mark came up on the electronic scoreboard, one by one. Five point six, five point four, five point five...hey, these marks looked good enough for third or fourth place, I thought. Sure enough, after the final skater had finished his program our team leader came rushing up.

"Hey, Jimmy! I just saw the results on the computer. You got third. A bronze medal!"

"Whoopee!" I yelled out. "What a great start. And just imagine how well you'll do when you calm down a little."

Jimmy smiled, and looked greatly relieved.

"Thanks, Charlie. I can see I've still got a lot to learn."

"You'll be fine, Jimmy. You've got the potential to become a great skater, but I think you realized today that you've got be a hundred and one percent ready for your competitions. Then you'll be more relaxed, mentally."

As we walked back to the dressing rooms, one of the competition officials came up to us.

"So, Mr. Donovan, you will please come with me for the drug testing procedure. The room is just down at the end of the hall."

"What?" said Jimmy.

"Oh, Jimmy," I said, in a reassuring voice. "I didn't have time to tell you about all the things that happen at these International events. This is normal procedure. They just take a urine sample from the top three finishers, plus one random skater. Then they send it to the laboratories to be tested, just to make sure you guys haven't been taking something you shouldn't have."

"But...do I have to? I mean..."

"Don't worry about it, Jimmy. But you might have to drink quite a lot of water first, to give them the sample. Skaters get very dehydrated after they've competed, and have very little fluid left in their bodies. Sometimes it would take me an hour, drinking about six bottles of water. And you can't leave the room until you've produced, otherwise you'll be disqualified."

Jimmy reluctantly followed the man into the medical area, and, sure enough, didn't come out for about an hour.

For the rest of the time that we were in Vienna, Jimmy became very quiet, almost to the point of being unsocial. I just put it down to the fact that he was a little overwhelmed with the whole occasion. After all, he'd hardly ever been away from home, and probably felt like a fish out of water. I could imagine how he felt, so, throughout the trip I'd tried to be like a father to him, as well as a coach.

We arrived home to great excitement. Both Jimmy's parents, and my own, were there to meet us at the airport. You'd have thought Jimmy had won a gold medal, the way his parents greeted him. They were jumping up and down when they saw us come out of the baggage claim area, and rushed forward to hug and kiss him. Well, his mother did, anyway.

My parents were somewhat calmer, but were, nevertheless, very glad to see me.

"Charlie!" my mother called out when she saw me. "It's so lovely to see you home safe again."

"Thanks. Well, mum and dad, It looks like I can still be a success." I said, as we hugged.

"Well, Jimmy," I said, turning to my budding star, "This has been a great start to your international career, but I suggest you take a few days off before we start back training for the next event. And, well done! I'm really proud of you."

"Thanks, Charlie. You're the best!"

We drove home in great spirits, and I spent the whole evening telling my parents about Vienna and the competition. Unfortunately, there was no way of foreseeing what was going to happen a couple of days later.

6

TROUBLE REARS ITS UGLY HEAD

"Charlie?" my mother called out. "There's a Mr. Spencer on the phone. Isn't he the President of the association?"

"Yes. I wonder what he wants? Must be pretty important if he's calling."

I went into the living room and picked up the phone.

"Hello? Mr. Spencer? This is an unexpected pleasure. What can I do for you?"

"Charlie, I have some rather unpleasant news for you, so I'll come straight to the point. We've just had a communication from the International Skating Union, telling us that your skater, Jimmy Donovan, has tested positive for methamphetamine use at the Vienna competition. I'm sure you know that methamphetamines are performance-enhancing drugs, therefore this is an extremely serious matter, and we, at the association, will be holding an inquiry as soon as possible to get all the facts. It's mandatory that you attend, and I would ask you to say nothing to the press, or, indeed, to anyone else, for that matter. We'll let you know as soon as we have a date for the inquiry."

"Yes...yes Mr. Spencer. I understand...but I can't believe this. Are they sure they got the test right? Surely this can't be true? Jimmy wouldn't do a thing like that."

"Well, I didn't want to believe it myself, but they've double-checked, and said there can be no mistake."

"Okay. Thank you for calling. I'll wait 'til I hear from you."

I put down the phone and, once again, felt numb.

My mother came into the room.

"You look as white as a ghost!"

"Yes, that *was* Mr. Spencer, from the skating association. He just told me that the I.S.U. informed him that Jimmy had tested positive for taking a performance-enhancing drug in Vienna."

"Oh, my goodness!" said mother, aghast.

"What an idiot. What a stupid idiot!" I said, feeling my blood starting to boil. "What was he thinking of? He's got such a bright future, and now he's blown it! The stupid, stupid idiot. Oh, my God!"

"Charlie. Please try to calm down. I'm sure it's not true, and that there's been a mistake. Don't get yourself all worked up for nothing. Please, Charlie."

"Oh, mum, you don't understand. If it *is* true, and it probably is, then not only has he ruined his career, but, and I know this sounds selfish, I've lost the chance to make a great start to *my* new career as a coach. You know, I *knew* there was something a bit different about Jimmy these past few weeks, but I couldn't put my finger on it. The way he's been all fired up and jumpy. And he told me the difference in him was his new diet. Phooey! Anyway, I'm going to call him now, and find out what he has to say for himself."

I picked up the phone and dialed his number. No answer. Over the next two hours I tried six more times, but again, no answer.

The next day I resumed teaching my lessons at the rink, and realized how wonderful it was to teach the local kids in a no-pressure situation. They just wanted to have fun, and I tried hard to oblige.

"Hey, Billy." I called out, to one of my students. "I want you to jump high, but when you do, mind the lights!"

For a few seconds he looked at me, incredulously, and then suddenly smiled when he realized I was joking. I was trying to have fun with the kids, but it was hard to keep my mind on my job. I just kept on thinking about Jimmy's stupid actions, and the upcoming inquiry.

That evening Mr. Spencer called back.

"Charlie. The inquiry is to be held at the skating association's headquarters next Monday at 10am. Try to be there a little earlier if you can, because we want to start on time. We have a lot to go through."

"Okay, Mr. Spencer. I'll be there in plenty of time."

That evening, after dinner, my mother and father noticed that I was very quiet.

"What's on your mind, Charlie." said my father.

"Oh, I don't know, dad. I've just got a bad feeling about this inquiry. And things were just starting to go well for me. Why can't life just run smoothly?"

"Well, Charlie, that's how life goes, sometimes. But I must admit, you've had more than your fair share of bad luck recently. So you'll just have to try to keep a level head, and we'll see how it turns out."

7

A Nasty Surprise

~~~) C ~~~

At precisely ten a.m., the next Monday morning, the secretary got up from her desk, opened the large doors in front of us, and ushered us into the wood-paneled meeting room at Ice Skating headquarters.

One of the association's employees came over to us.

"Mr. Williams, will you please sit on that side of the table, and Jimmy, would you sit over there."

We duly obliged.

Once everyone was seated, Mr. Spencer took a document out of his briefcase and started to read it.

"The purpose of this inquiry is to assess the situation of a skater, representing Great Britain in a Junior International event in Vienna, who has tested positive for taking a methamphetamine performance-enhancing drug. As you may well imagine, the image of British ice skating will be under close scrutiny by the media, so it's important that this matter doesn't get blown out of proportion.

Those present are as follows: James Donovan, the skater in question. His coach, Charles Williams. Emily Stoddart, stenographer, five members of the Disciplinary committee, namely: John Briggs, Clare Larson, Edward Barraclough, Peter Oldham, John Matlow, and myself, Philip Spencer, President. I will open by reading the report of the drug test taken at the Vienna competition."

We all listened intently as Philip Spencer carefully read out the report. It sounded very serious and, worse still, very damaging. Jimmy looked like he was in big trouble, but I was quite unprepared for the bombshell that was about to explode.

The President looked Jimmy square in the eye and asked,

"Jimmy, do you admit that you took methamphetamines in the hope that they would improve your performance?"

"Yes, I admit it, but it wasn't my idea."

"What do you mean by that?"

"My coach, Charlie Williams, gave them to me. He said they would make me perform much better."

"WHAT?" I yelled out. "What are you saying, Jimmy?"

"Mr. Williams!" called out Mr. Spencer. "Will you please sit down and be quiet."

"But this isn't true! Jimmy, why are you saying this? Why are you lying?"

Not being able to look me in the face, Jimmy looked down at the table as he stammered,

"You...you know you gave them to me. You said I'd need them to be able to perform well. I didn't want to take them."

"You're a liar, Jimmy!"

"Mr. Williams. Will you please stop accusing your pupil. Can't you see he's extremely upset. You'll have your chance to speak later."

"But this isn't fair. I wouldn't even know where to get hold of a drug like that. I'm totally opposed to drugs."

"As I said, Mr. Williams, you'll have your chance to speak later. Now, Jimmy, when and where is he supposed to have given you these drugs?"

"It was in the rink one morning. I wasn't skating very well, and he said that he could give me something that would give me a real 'lift', and make me skate much better. I said I wasn't sure if I should, but he said, 'Oh, just take some and don't tell anybody about it.' Well, I did, and within two days I started to feel bolder in my skating, so he told me to keep taking them. Now, I feel like he's got me addicted to them."

It was all I could do to stop myself reaching across the table to wring his neck. My blood was boiling, and I had to bite my tongue to stop myself from yelling at him. What a conniving little slime-ball, I thought.

"Well now, Jimmy." reassured Philip Spencer. "You do realize you've done something very wrong, but if it is the decision of the disciplinary committee that you were coerced into taking these drugs by your coach, then these mitigating circumstances may be taken into consideration by the International Skating Union, and this could result in a significant reduction on the length of the ban they impose on you. Do you understand what I'm saying?"

"Yes, thank you, sir. I do."

Philip Spencer turned his head, and looked in my direction.

"Now then, Mr. Williams. Did you, or did you not, give methamphetamine drugs to your pupil, Jimmy Donovan?"

"No, I did not!"

"So you are calling your pupil a liar?"

"Yes I am. And a filthy little scheming one, too!"

"Really, Mr. Williams! I think it would be better for you if you kept your emotions under control."

"I'm sorry. But this is just too much. I'm innocent of his accusations."

"What were your ambitions when you started coaching?"

"I just wanted to enjoy teaching the young kids, and try to be a role model to them by showing them that they should do things the right way, and have good morals."

"You would, in fact, want them to follow the good examples you would be setting?"

"Yes. That's right, Mr. Spencer."

"But Mr. Williams. Did you, or did you not, say in a telephone conversation with Steve Collins, that you, and I quote, *were going to do anything you had to, to be a successful coach*'?"

"Well...I didn't mean I'd do anything bad."

"Mr. Williams, the newspapers made it quite clear that your career-ending injury left you extremely frustrated, and very bitter. Could this have led you to the extreme measure of persuading your pupil to take this drug, in order for you to find some consolation in *his* success?"

I stood up, and leaned forward across the table.

"Why don't you listen to me?" I shouted, feeling my heart racing. "I didn't give him any drug. He's lying!"

"Mr. Williams. Unless you calm down, we shall have to have you removed from this inquiry, and you will forfeit your remaining opportunity to present your case."

I slumped back into my chair. I couldn't believe the way I was being treated. Just a few months before, most of the people in this room were congratulating me, patting me on the back, and shaking my hand. Amazing, isn't it, how the world turns?

There were a few more formal questions asked of Jimmy and myself, and then Philip Spencer announced,

"I think we've covered everything, so I would now like everyone but the members of the disciplinary committee to leave the room and wait outside. We'll call you back in when we've decided what action will be taken. I shouldn't think this will take more than twenty or thirty minutes, so please be patient."

We filed out and sat down on the chairs in the hall. All except Jimmy, that is. He walked down the hall as far as he could, clearly trying to distance himself from me.

It seemed like an eternity before they called us back in, and, by the look on the faces of the disciplinary committee, someone was in serious trouble. They first addressed Jimmy.

"Clearly, by your admittance, and the findings of the International Skating Union, you have violated the rules of ice skating, and will be banned from competing for a period of time to be determined by the disciplinary committee. You will be kept informed about this in the near future. However, we find that there are mitigating circumstances, and we will take these into consideration when deciding the length of the ban."

Then, all eyes turned to me.

"Mr. Williams. After discussing this matter very carefully, it is our belief that you took advantage of your position of trust, and encouraged your skater, James Donovan, to take a performance-enhancing drug. By doing this, you knowingly contravened the rules of ice skating."

"But..." I started to speak. "You really don't have the true facts. I mean..."

Philip Spencer wouldn't even let me finish the sentence.

"We feel that your whole character has changed since your accident, and that you would only be a bad influence on young skaters, were you to be allowed to continue teaching. Therefore, you are hereby banned from the Skating Association. We're sorry, Mr. Williams, but our decision is final."

I felt as though I was having a nightmare, and that I would suddenly wake up and it would all be just a bad dream. But it wasn't. This was really happening to me.

I knew it wasn't the right thing to do, but I got up from my chair and left the room without saying another word. There was no point in pleading my case, or making any sort of appeal. Jimmy had clearly fooled the committee, and I was about to hit rock bottom.

I arrived home about an hour later, and broke the news to my parents. My father nearly hit the roof.

"I can't believe it! The little beggar! And after all you've done for him. Well don't you worry, Charlie, he'll get his come-uppance, you'll see."

"Yes, but that doesn't solve my problem. My whole coaching career has fallen apart, so what do I do now?"

"Try and get a goodnight's sleep, son. And then we'll talk about it tomorrow."

Well, the next morning came, and all hell broke loose. It was definitely a case of 'out of the frying pan and into the fire'. Our next door neighbor, George Harper, called out from his front garden, at the top of his voice,

"Have you seen the headlines in the sports sections of the newspapers, Charlie? What's this all about?"

I stuck my head out of my bedroom window.

"George! You don't have to tell the whole neighborhood."

"I'm afraid they already know, Charlie."

"Oh, dear. In that case, come in and have a cup of tea, George, and I'll tell you a story. The only trouble is, I don't know the ending, yet."

George came into the kitchen, and we all sat down.

"Here you are, George." said my mother, handing him a cup of tea.

"Ooh, lovely!" he replied, making a loud slurping noise as he drank it. "You make the best cuppa in the world."

"Thank you, George. So what do you think of all this terrible business?"

"Oh, it's disgusting, the way they've gone for Charlie. Everyone in the neighborhood knows he wouldn't do a thing like that."

"Ah, thank you, George." I said, managing my first smile in days. "That really is comforting to know."

George was genuinely concerned for me. He was that sort of person. The salt of the earth, in fact. He was not a handsome man - not on the outside, at least - and had never married, but he'd been our next door neighbor for as long as I can remember, living by himself in his own private world. There was nothing he wouldn't do for his friends and neighbors.

A few years ago, he volunteered to wash our upstairs windows from the outside. He was almost finished, when he fell off his ladder and took quite a bad fall. When we rushed over to him, he jumped up and said, "Oh, don't worry. I'm fine." It turned out, though, that he had a badly sprained wrist.

"Well, Charlie, I must be off now. Thanks for the tea."

"Our pleasure, George. And thanks for the kind words."

After breakfast, I decided to go for a long walk. I needed to do some serious thinking. Probably the most serious thinking of my life, so far. My whole future was at stake, and I couldn't afford to make any wrong decisions. I walked the mile or so to the park where I used to play as a child, because I always felt a warmth and security there. By the time I got home later that day, I knew what I had to do.

I found my mother in the kitchen, chopping up some vegetables.

"Hello, mum. What time's dinner?"

"In about 30 minutes. Dad should be home by then."

Then she put down her knife, and turned to me.

"This has been devastating for you, hasn't it?"

"Yeah. I still can't believe how he tried to blame me."

"We know you didn't give him any drugs, Charlie,' said my mother, in a comforting tone. "Your dad and I have complete faith in you."

"I know you do, mum. But it looks pretty bad for me. Jimmy spun a convincing yarn to the press, and they swallowed every bit of it. So did the skating association, so my name's mud, now."

Mum put her arm around my shoulder. "Well, then. Have you thought about what you might want to do?"

"Well," I replied, "Skating is all I know. The problem is, I won't be able to get a job anywhere in England without the finger being pointed at me. No-one's going to take lessons from me, now. I'm poison. And just when I was beginning to like coaching."

Mum sighed, and turned to carry on preparing dinner, while I went into the living room and slumped down onto the sofa to do some more thinking.

It was beginning to dawn on me that, if I wanted to continue teaching, I would have to leave the country. Other coaches had done it and been very successful, but, somehow, it didn't seem like something I would do. And the more I thought about it, the more I realized what a nice, secure home life I'd had, with hardly a worry in the world. No bills to pay, a meal always ready on the table, and the undying love and support of my parents. I supposed one day I would have to go out on my own, but now it had become reality. I wasn't ready for this.

It didn't seem very long before my mother called out,

"Dinner's ready! Dad just came home, so come in and sit down."

The three of us sat down and, in between mouthfuls, I started to tell my parents what was on my mind.

"You know, I've decided that I don't even want to try and find work in another English ice rink. With all this bad publicity, I'm too embarrassed to go 'cap-in-hand' to all the rink managers. No, I've got to think about moving to another country if I want to keep teaching."

"Oh, Charlie. We'd miss you so much if you left home." said my mother.

"Well, mum. If I was getting married I'd be leaving home, anyway. And even if I wasn't, I'd be going sometime."

"I know, Charlie. But it would be under better circumstances."

"And then, look at the newspaper headlines." I pointed out. "Even though I'm innocent, it must be so embarrassing for you, my parents, to be connected with this. I'm so ashamed that this is happening to you. You never deserved this, but one day I'll make them eat their words."

"You wouldn't think Jimmy could do something so nasty, would you?" said my mother.

"But he did. He lied. You must believe me. I need to know that you believe me."

"We do, son." said my father. "But I can't understand why the lad told such lies?"

"He was scared, and just tried to wriggle his way out of a bad situation." I replied. "Anyway, I'll telephone Herr Schnabel tomorrow. He may know of a good teaching position in Germany. And, mum, Germany's only a two hour flight from England, so it would be easy for me to fly home now and again."

Father thought for a moment, put down his knife and fork, and then said quietly,

"Well, son. I think it's a very brave decision you're making. Of course, it's one you shouldn't be having to make, but there it is. You never know what life's going to throw at you from day to day, but we know you'll make the right decision. So you think Germany might be a good place to start?"

"Yes, because I know a lot of people over there, and I won't feel like a stranger. I know a few German words, too, so I'd be able to communicate with the skaters without too much difficulty."

"And I've heard the German beer is almost as good as ours!" Dad joked.

We finished our dinner, and I felt a little bit better knowing that I was going to be talking to some friends the next day.

After a good night's sleep, and one of my mother's substantial breakfasts, I got on the phone to Herr Schnabel.

"Hello? Herr Schnabel? This is Charlie Williams, calling from London."

"Oh...Charlie. Yes...how are you?"

"Oh, I'm fine, thank you. And you?"

"Er...well, I'm fine, too."

"That's good. The reason I'm calling you is that I've been thinking about teaching in Germany, and, of course, you're the first person I wanted to call to see if you know of any positions that might be open. You know everything that's going on in your country."

"Charlie..." he replied, in a very somber tone. "I'm afraid you're not going to have much success finding a job here in Germany. You see, news travels fast in the skating world, and everyone has heard about you."

"But, Herr Schnabel, it's all lies! I'm innocent...really. I never supplied him with drugs."

"Well, Charlie, if you say that, then I believe you. But my belief in your innocence won't help you here. The German skating association is very strict on substance abuse, and you would not be allowed to teach anywhere."

"Oh, my God. I thought I'd be able to get away from this nightmare, and still have something to look forward to, but maybe it's not going to be so easy."

"No, I'm sorry Charlie, I don't think it's going to be that easy for you."

We said our 'goodbyes', and I put down the phone. No, this wasn't going to be easy.

They say bad news travels fast, and where I was concerned, it traveled at the speed of light. Further calls to France, Sweden, and Italy confirmed the fact that I had little hope of securing a teaching position anywhere in Europe. Everywhere I called, it was a case of, "Thanks, but no thanks."

I went into the kitchen and relayed the bad news to my parents.

"It seems like I'm going to have to go to the ends of the earth to escape from this terrible cloud that's hanging over me. I mean, the word's got all around Europe about what's happened. Now it seems like I'd have to go to the other side of the planet to get a job where, maybe, they haven't heard about me. Wait a minute...that may not be such a bad idea."

"What do you mean, Charlie?" mum asked.

"Well, what have I got to lose? I *could* go to the other side of the world. Australia, maybe. They speak English, so there wouldn't be any language problem.

I pondered that thought for a while.

"Hang on a minute. I've got an idea, mum."

I ran upstairs to my room and searched for the frequent flyer statements from the airlines I'd been flying on. When I found them, I took them downstairs and laid them out on the kitchen table.

"There you are, mum, it's what I thought. I've accumulated more than enough miles to get a free round trip to Australia, so all these years of traveling to international competitions haven't gone to waste, after all. If nothing else, I'll have a nice little holiday to help me forget my problems. And Australia might be just the place for me. A fresh start, and all that, y'know?"

"Ooh, Charlie. That's so far away. Get back on the phone and try France and Germany again, will you?"

"Oh, mum. You've got no sense of adventure."

"Me? What about your dad? He thinks it's a huge adventure driving down to Brighton for the day!"

I didn't think I could laugh, but that remark made me giggle a bit.

"Well, at least I still have Cindy in my life. Maybe I can visit her on the way back."

In the following few days I made a few more calls, but to no avail. I was being treated like a leper, but before I made any final decisions about traveling, I thought I'd try Jimmy just one more time. His phone just kept ringing, and then his answering machine turned on. I decided to leave a message.

"Jimmy, this is Charlie. Look...I don't think you realize it, but you've just about ruined my life with these lies. And even now, I should be really angry with you, but I'm not, because I know you only did it because you were scared, and couldn't find a way out. But you can't go through life passing the blame onto someone else when you make a mistake. We all make mistakes, but we have to try and take responsibility for them. Please call me, and maybe we can clear up this mess in a way that hurts neither of us."

More days passed, and it then became obvious to me that he wasn't going to reply. Maybe he wanted to, but wasn't allowed to by his parents. I would never find out.

A couple of days later, I was sitting at the dinner table, feeling pretty low in spirits.

"You know, mum and dad, I think I *will* use those frequent flyer miles to take a trip to Australia. So, after dinner, I'm going to write to Cindy and tell her that I can come and see her on my way back. She'll be so excited, and I'm already feeling a bit better just thinking about the trip."

"Oh, I almost forgot to tell you, Charlie." said my mother. "There's a letter from her on the hall table."

"Oh, boy!" I exclaimed. "A letter from Cindy is just the tonic I need to lift my spirits".

I rushed out to the hall and picked up the letter. On my way back to the kitchen I opened it, and started reading.

"What's the matter, Charlie? You look like you've seen a ghost." said my mother.

I dropped the letter on the table.

"Oh, my God!" I groaned. "I didn't think the news would reach America."

My father picked up the letter and started reading it.

"What does it say?" inquired my mother.

He read it out aloud.

"Charlie. I've just seen the newspapers! I know how much you wanted to be successful, but I can't believe you could stoop this low. I'm so disappointed in you. I was going to phone you, but then I realized I never want to hear your voice, or see you, again. Don't try to contact me. I won't answer. Goodbye."

Well, that did it. The last straw. How can a person's life go from such a 'high', to such a 'low' in such a short space of time? Now I had nothing to lose by going to Australia. Just about everything in my life had fallen apart, so it was definitely time to seek new horizons.

It only took me a few hours to get my air ticket and pack my bags. I never thought I would be in such a rush to leave my beloved country, but I had to get away from this nightmare as soon as possible.

Later that evening the phone rang.

"Hello," I said. "Who is it?"

"It's Don Hastings, you old party-pooper. I just called to see how you're doing?"

"Oh, I'm okay thanks, Don. It's nice to hear from you. I didn't think I had any friends left."

"Oh, don't worry about that. All of us at the rink know you're completely innocent. In fact, we all want to have a good old get-together with you, and take you out to dinner this weekend. How about it?"

"You're not going to believe this, Don, but I'm going to have to take another rain check. You see, I leave for Australia on Friday."

"You what??"

"I'm afraid so, Don. And I'll miss you. You've been a good buddy, but I can't take this pressure any more. I feel like I'm living a nightmare, and this is the only way to escape from it."

"Well, that a great shame, Charlie, because you're the victim of a bad situation. I don't know whether you knew this, but we'd heard that Jimmy's dad gives him a real beating if he does anything wrong, so he was between a rock and a hard place when it came to taking the blame for the drug incident. He had to make up that lie about you because he was afraid of getting another beating from his father."

"Oh, my God, Don, I had no idea that was going on."

"Oh, yes. This had been going on for a long time, and it was only a matter of time before something bad happened. But, listen, Charlie, I was also calling to tell you to call Miss Cook. I know she'd like to hear from you, but she's too proud to make the first move."

"Well, if you really think so."

"Talk to her, Charlie. She believes in you, and may still have some good advice for you."

"Thanks, Don, I will. And I'll call you as soon as I'm back, so we can finally get together for that drink!"

"Okay, Charlie. Safe journey, and, talk to you later. Keep in touch."

I put down the phone and thought for a moment. What if I call Miss Cook and she's angry with me? I don't think I could cope with that. Then again, what have I got to lose? I dialed her number.

"Hello, Miss Cook? It's Charlie. Charlie Williams."

"Hello, chum. How are you?"

"Well, as well as can be expected. I'm sure you've heard all about it."

"Yes, I've been following the news, and it's most unfortunate. But don't worry, Charlie. I've known you for quite a few years, and I think

I'm a good judge of character. I know you wouldn't have got involved with drugs."

"Thanks, Miss Cook. It means a lot to know that you still have faith in me. But, as you can imagine, I don't feel very good about the fact that I can't teach in England any more, and, as most European countries don't want me either, I'm going to try my luck in Australia. I leave on Friday."

"Oh, I'm sorry to hear that. But I'm sure you know the skating world's a very small one, so word about you got around very quickly. It can be quite cruel out there, Charlie, and you'll find that you'll need to look over your shoulder every now and then. Teaching can be very rewarding, but there's always a certain amount of jealousy and back-stabbing going on in this sport, so look after yourself."

"Thanks, Miss Cook, I will. And thanks for that good advice. I was afraid to call you, but I'm glad I did, now, because I feel much better now that I've talked to you."

"Alright, chum. I'm glad you called, too. Keep in touch, and let me know how you're doing."

I thought she was going to hang up the phone, but then she added,

"I wouldn't say this to many pupils, Charlie, but I'll miss seeing you at the rink. I never had any children, and so I have to say that I've envied your mother on more than one occasion. You were always a well-mannered boy, and tried hard in your lessons. A coach can't ask for much more than that. Take good care of yourself...and good luck."

And with that, she did hang up.

After I put down the phone, my emotions welled up inside me, and I was glad no-one was around for a few minutes.

The evening before I left, I sat down to dinner with my mother and father, and tried to keep things from being too serious.

"So, mum and dad, I'm only going to be away for two weeks, so it's really just a vacation. That's the best way to look at it."

"You mean this isn't the 'last supper', then?" said my smiling father.

"No, dad. Not likely. I couldn't exist without mum's great cooking. You know, Australia's full of English people, but I bet not one of them can do 'Bangers and Mash' like you can, mum."

"Oh, thanks, Charlie. I'll have a big plate of them ready for you when you come home."

After dinner, I went up to my bedroom and finished packing my suitcases. As tired as I was, though, I didn't sleep much that night. There were just too many things on my mind. In less than a week my life had completely changed, and I realized I should never take anything for granted. From now on, I was always going to be prepared for the unexpected. I had learned one of life's lessons, and, if anything, it had toughened me up a bit. A toughness that was going to stand me in good stead in the future.

The morning came a little too soon for my liking, and I was still very sleepy when my mother brought a cup of tea up to my bedroom.

"Here you are, Charlie." she said, brightly. "This'll get your motor running."

My motor felt like it had a flat battery, but I drank the tea and then hauled myself out of bed to get ready. I always found that a nice hot shower woke me up better than anything else, and by the time I got downstairs I was ready to take on the world. And, of course, a nice big English breakfast didn't hurt, either.

"Well, son," said my father, picking up my two suitcases, "We'd better get going."

There was an ominous light drizzle that added a tinge of sadness to the occasion, and we drove out to Heathrow Airport in almost complete silence. Halfway there, I started to have misgivings. Oh, my God, I thought. What am I doing? Do I really want to go? But, a few seconds later, common sense prevailed, and I made myself realize that I should be looking forward to what could turn out to be quite an exciting adventure.

Instead of dropping me off at the terminal and going straight home again, my father decided to park the car so that he and my mother could sit with me in the airport until the flight was called. The problem was, none of us had bargained for the frenzied scene that was about to take place.

As soon as I got into the terminal, press reporters and photographers seemed to come out of nowhere, and closed in on me like vultures. All I wanted was a quiet moment with my parents to say goodbye, but the unrelenting members of the press pestered us, and hounded us all the way to the departure lounge. They couldn't give a damn about our feelings, as long as they got their story and pictures.

"I'm sorry, mum and dad." I said, shaking my head in despair. "I thought at least we'd have some peace and quiet here."

My mother shrugged her shoulders and said,

"That's alright, Charlie. It's still nice to be here to see you off."

But as soon as she'd got those words out, she couldn't hold back her emotions any longer. Tears started streaming down her cheeks, and she hugged me like she never wanted to let go.

"Oh, Charlie, Charlie…" she cried. "Will I really see you back here again in a couple of weeks?"

When she said that, even dad couldn't hold back his tears, and he held us both in a group hug.

"Of course I'll be back." I said, reassuringly.

The photographers closed in for the kill. Snap, snap, snap, went their cameras, as they made sure they captured the sadness on my parent's faces.

"Can't you people go away." I pleaded, but it didn't stop them.

A few seconds later, we heard an announcement.

"Passengers for Flight 002 to Sydney should now proceed to Gate 41 for boarding."

"That's me, mum and dad. Gotta go. Thanks for everything, and I'll see you in a couple of weeks."

"Have a good time, son. Your mum and I will miss you while you're gone."

"I'll miss you, too."

As I waved goodbye to my parents, two reporters called out,

"Do you have anything to say, Charlie?"

"Do you think you've got any future if you come back to England?"

At first, I ignored their heartless remarks and started walking towards the gate, but then I turned and said,

"Yes, I do have something to say. The damage caused by this terrible business is irreparable. But I pray that, one day, the truth will come out. I'm innocent."

8

NEW HORIZONS

~⁓) (⁓~

I had no idea airliners could stay in the air for so long. The total travel time was about twenty-three hours, with a brief stop in Singapore, and it seemed an eternity before we finally touched down at Kingsford-Smith International Airport in Sydney.

I felt a pang of excitement as the plane taxied up to the gate. After all, I was on the other side of the world, and had no idea what was in store for me.

Getting through immigration and customs took no time at all, and I was soon being whisked into downtown Sydney in a taxi driven by a budding grand prix driver. He switched lanes, cut corners, and got me to my hotel in what he called record time. If that was the case, I hoped his next passenger had a strong stomach in anticipation of another record-breaking run.

Check-in didn't take very long, fortunately, because as soon as I got into my room the jet lag hit me, and I just slumped onto the bed and fell sound asleep.

Ten hours later I woke up feeling pretty groggy, but after a nice hot shower and a big Australian breakfast I was ready to do a little sightseeing.

Day one, and my first stop had to be Bondi beach. A beach that most British folk can only dream of. And here I was, standing near the water's edge, with the powdery white sand between my toes. Fantastic! And, interestingly, Bondi beach is a favorite place to be on Christmas day because this is the southern hemisphere, and our winter is their summer. I don't think I could get used to that.

Next stop was the Sydney Opera House. A marvel of modern architecture, situated right on the harbor. Then, it was back to the hotel for a nice dinner and a stroll around the neighborhood before turning in for the night.

The next day, I visited 'The Rocks', which I was told was the foundation of Sydney, and Australia, and was of enormous historical significance. Then, to finish up with, a walk around the 'Chinese Garden of Friendship', not far from Chinatown.

Day three arrived, and I decided I'd had enough fun, so it was time to get down to business. I looked up some numbers in the phone book and started making some calls.

"Good morning...yes, could I speak to the manager, please."

"Just one moment. Putting you through."

"This is the manager. Can I help you?"

"Yes, I've just moved to this country, and I wondered if you had an opening for a coach?"

"No, I'm sorry. I wish I could help you, but I've got a full coaching staff, here. Some of the other rinks in Sydney might be able to help you, though. Give them a call."

I did give them a call, and it was the same answer at every rink. 'Sorry, but we're full'.

I don't think they knew who was calling, so I knew they weren't just giving me the brush-off. It was just that the rinks had all the staff they needed.

Right. Next stop, Melbourne.

Apart from the fact that Melbourne was a totally different city, inasmuch as it was quaint, Victorian, and much more conservative than cosmopolitan Sydney, it was definitely a case of déjà vu. I checked into a hotel, I saw all the sights, and got a negative response from every ice rink I called. All in all, a very depressing situation. It wasn't going to solve any problems, but a cold beer seemed like a good idea at that moment, so I went out of the hotel to find a friendly pub.

As I was walking past a restaurant, feeling as fed up as I can ever remember, I heard the words of a song playing on a radio, "Take a long trip to nowhere...etc. etc."

I stopped in my tracks and thought for a second. Why not? What have I got to lose? I had a quick beer, and then went straight back to the hotel and checked out.

"Can you get me a taxi, please?" I asked the desk clerk.

"Certainly, sir. Where shall I tell him you're going?"

"The bus station."

When I got there, I took a look at one of the timetables, and randomly picked out the name of a town. And, I only bought a one-way ticket. This, I thought to myself, was totally insane, but hey, don't we all have an insane moment at some time in our lives?

The particular bus I was going to travel on was leaving in about ten minutes, so I hurriedly bought a couple of soft drinks and potato chips, and boarded without delay. Sure enough, five minutes later the driver started up the engine and off we went.

As we left the downtown area and started going through the suburbs, I wished I had seen more of Melbourne, but it was too late now, so I reclined my seat and cast my thoughts back to the sights I had seen in both great cities. At least I would have those memories to cherish forever.

About an hour later, we made our first stop. Quite a few passengers got off at this point, leaving about six of us to continue our journey. We were now well out of the city, and heading into what seemed like a wilderness.

Another hour went by. Just when it seemed like we were never going to stop, the bus began slowing down, and then pulled off the road.

"Pengellan Rest Stop," announced the driver. "I'd take advantage of it if I were you, because it's five more hours until we reach out final stop. You can get some decent coffee and sandwiches inside."

The six of us filed out into the warm evening air and enjoyed stretching our legs.

"Blimey," said one of them, wiping his brow. "It's going to be a hot one tomorrow."

"How can you tell?" I asked.

"Oh, the dryness of the air...and that red glow on the horizon. Yeah, it'll be 105, maybe."

I'd been mistakenly thinking I was in a cool area, having been lulled into a false sense of security by the air conditioning on the bus.

"Yes, well," I replied. "I'm going to get some food to take on the bus. Sounds like I'll have plenty of time to eat it."

A few minutes later, we were all back in our seats for the final leg of this mystery trip. A mystery trip for me, anyway.

For the next five hours the incessant drone of the engine was only broken up by the occasional gear change as we started to go up, or down, a hill. On and on we went into the darkness. I finished my sandwiches and coffee, and reclined the seat. What on earth am I doing on this road to nowhere, I thought to myself, as I closed my eyes.

I must have slept for about two hours, when I felt someone tap me on the shoulder.

"Wake up, mate, said the driver. "End of the line."

"Where are we?"

"Warragong Springs, mate. Gateway to nowhere!"

"Oh, thanks."

As I stepped off the bus, a young man picked up my suitcases.

"Where to, mate? The Warragong Springs Hotel?"

"What other hotels are there?" I asked.

"There aren't. That's the only one. But it's a five star hotel, mate, and you can see four of them through the hole in the roof!"

I laughed.

"No jokin' though, really." he went on. "We're known as the little town with the big heart. Actually, we're not such a small town. You can find everything here. We even have a cinema." he said, proudly.

"Wow," I thought, sarcastically.

We stopped to shake hands.

"My name's Charlie Williams. What's yours?"

"Billy. Billy Cameron."

"And what do you do, Billy?"

"Well, my real jobs are running the 'Crazy Kangaroo' bar down the street from the hotel, and driving the Zamboni at the ice rink."

I stopped in my tracks. "There's an ice rink...here?" I asked, incredulously.

"Oh, yes," Billy replied. "Some rich bloke built it a few years ago just for a hobby, and then just left town when he got bored with it. Mr. Johnson's the new owner, now."

"In that case, I'll get a good night's sleep, and go and see him in the morning. You see, I teach ice skating."

It took us about five or six minutes to walk to the hotel, and it felt good after sitting on that bus for so many hours. Billy led the way into the lobby and put down my suitcases. I reached into my pocket and gave him a couple of dollars.

"Thanks, Charlie. Much obliged. I hope I'll see you around, then?"

"If you work at the ice rink, you'll definitely be seeing me very soon."

Checking in, I asked the hotel clerk what rooms he had.

"Well, I can give you rooms with four different views: Looking out onto the main street, the side streets to the north or south, or the alley at the back. What do you fancy?"

"Oh, definitely the view out onto the main street." I replied. "I want to see everything that's going on."

It didn't take me very long to unpack, and as soon as I'd finished I went straight to bed.

The next morning, I fortified myself with a good breakfast, and headed for the ice rink.

On my way there, everybody I met was friendly, and helpful with directions. It was good to see smiles on faces, instead of frowns. Once there, I sought out the manager's office, and knocked on the door.

"Yes...come in," said a loud voice from inside.

My heart skipped a beat. "Er...Mr. Johnson?"

"Yes. Ralph Johnson." he replied, reaching out to shake hands. "What can I do for you?"

"Well, I've just arrived in town, and wondered if there might be a teaching position here at your rink?"

"Come and sit down and let's talk about it."

I pulled up a chair near his desk, and took a deep breath.

He leaned back in his chair and eyed me up and down. Then he looked at me quizzically.

"You're Charlie Williams, aren't you?"

"Er...yes. You know me?"

"Of course, mate," he said, cracking a smile. "We may be out in the middle of nowhere, but we do have television and magazines."

I felt a little red-faced, and found it hard to look him in the eye.

"So, Charlie. Why don't you tell me what a bloke like you is doing in a place like this."

"Well, Mr. Johnson, it's like this. You probably read about me having to stop competing, and how I started coaching. Well...I took over this really promising skater, and I thought that everything was rosy, but then he was tested for drugs at a competition, and was found positive for using a performance-enhancing substance. Honestly, Mr. Johnson, I had no idea he'd taken anything, but then, to try and get himself off the hook, he turned around and told the press, and the Skating Association, that *I'd* supplied it. And, because he put on such a convincing act, they believed him."

For a few seconds Mr. Johnson just sat there. Then he smiled.

"Charlie, I have no doubts about you, whatsoever. And I think everyone here will believe in you, too. We don't believe all that stuff in the newspapers, anyway, so here's what I want you to do. Get yourself settled down, and then, when you're ready, get stuck into a few lessons with some of the kids here, and we'll evaluate you in a month or so. I think you're going to like this place. Out here, Charlie, we judge a bloke by what he can do, not by his history. After all, it's the future that's important, isn't it?"

I laughed. "That's fine by me."

Mr. Johnson suggested getting some coffee out of the vending machine, and sitting by the side of the rink to watch the kids skate for a while.

We sat down and sipped our coffee.

"You have a nice group of kids here." I said.

"Yes, we're very proud of them. They work hard, and never give up trying. Trouble is, they haven't had any lessons for a while. I employed a guy called Wally Mulroney to coach here, but I had to fire him last month because he was drinking a bottle of beer for each lesson he taught, and, one day, he simply keeled over in the middle of the rink."

"Did you have to call the paramedics?" I asked.

"No," replied Mr. Johnson. "We just left him lying there. Then, at the end of the session, we pushed him off the ice with the Zamboni."

"You know," I said. "I think I'm going to like this place."

After we'd said our goodbyes, and I'd walked back to the hotel, I realized I needed to sit down and write a letter to my parents.

9

ANOTHER SECOND CHANCE!

~~~)(~~~

Dear Mum and Dad,

I hope you got the postcards I sent from Sydney and Melbourne. This whole trip still seems to be a bit of a dream, but I've ended up in a little town called Warragong Springs, about seven hours by bus from Melbourne. It's a small town, but everyone's very friendly, and it's just what I needed.

Now, please don't get upset, mum, but I'm going to stay here for a little while because, guess what? I've landed a job at the ice rink, and the owner, Mr. Johnson, is very happy to have me. And, he knows about what happened in England, and couldn't care less. He believes in me, and I feel like a new man, so I've got to give it a try. There are already several children here who are going to take lessons from me. Wish me luck!

    I hope you're both well, and I'll write again in a few days. I miss you both very much.

Love, Charlie.

That evening, I decided to go down to the 'Crazy Kangaroo' bar for a beer.

As soon as I walked in the door, I heard a familiar voice. It was Billy Cameron, serving drinks from behind the bar.

"Hello, Charlie! Come and have a beer. This one's on the house, but from tomorrow, you pay."

I laughed, and sat down at the bar.

"Thanks, Billy. That's very kind of you. You already make me feel at home."

"Well, from what I hear, it may *be* your home for at least a little while."

Then Billy called out at the top of his voice,

"Hey, everybody! I want you to meet our new ice skating coach. The one and only Charlie Williams!"

Everyone in the bar cheered, and then stood up and raised their glasses to me. One by one, they expressed their feelings.

"Here's to you, Charlie!"

"Best of luck, mate!"

"Good on ya, Cobber. You'll do us proud!"

"Can you teach me to skate to '*Waltzing Matilda*?"

"Come off it, Bruce. The only ice you've ever seen is in your drink."

And so it went on. Each one of them had a welcoming comment for me, or something funny to say. But, best of all, it was good to be among real people who made me feel wanted.

Billy came over and sat with me.

"Where are you going to stay? You can't live in a hotel if you're going to be with us for a while."

"No, I suppose not. I hadn't really thought about it, yet."

"No worries, then. You can stay with us. We've got a really nice spare room with it's own bathroom, and my mum and dad will make you feel right at home. And, it's within walking distance of the rink."

"That sounds great! But are you sure it'll be okay?"

"Of course, mate." said Billy, sounding chirpier than ever. "I'll pick you up at lunchtime, after you've done your morning lessons."

"Okay. Thanks, Billy. You're a real pal."

The next day, I couldn't have been more excited to get on the ice. I arrived much earlier than I needed to, but it gave me the chance to familiarize myself with the rink.

I thought I'd better get on the ice and skate around a bit, because it had been days since I'd skated, and I felt pretty stiff. After you've been used to training day in, day out, it really tells when you stay off the ice for more than a week, so I put on my skates and put in a few laps. It felt good to stretch out my body again, and I was soon performing some of my old maneuvers, minus, of course, any triple jumps.

As I stopped to catch my breath, I heard a round of applause from the side of the rink. Three of the local kids had the morning off school, and had also come to the rink early.

"Boy, you're good, Mister!" one of them yelled out.

"Why, thank you gentlemen." I replied, giving them a big theatrical bow.

Then, just for fun, I skated at full speed over to where they were standing, and sprayed them with snow from a powerful hockey stop.

"Hey! Stop it!" one of them cried.

"Blimey! Can you teach us to do that?" said another.

"Of course I can," I said. "I'm the new coach here. My name's Charlie. What's yours?"

"My name's Johnny." said the first one.

"My name's Johnny, too." said the second.

"And so is mine." said the third.

"Are you guys having me on?" I said, giving them a sideways look.

"No, Charlie." said the first one. "It's just that we all became friends a couple of years ago, and found out we all have the same name."

"So, doesn't it get confusing when you talk to each other, or someone calls you?"

"It did, until we gave ourselves some nicknames. Now, we each have our own identity."

"I think I'm going to regret this," I groaned. "But what are your nicknames?"

"Well," said the first one. "I'm 'Speedy', 'cos I can outrun the other two."

"And I'm 'Brains'", said the second. "'Cos I'm better than the other two at school."

I smiled.

"And you?" I asked the third one.

"Oh, I'm 'Munchy', 'cos I'm always eating something."

"Well, you'll never jump very high if you eat too much." I said.

"Oh, I don't usually eat when I'm skating."

"Well that's good news."

I thought I may as well make a start with them, so I told them to get their skates on and follow me onto the ice.

"Okay, boys. Now, to skate well you need good balance, body control, and confidence. And, a certain amount of intelligence doesn't hurt, either, because it's important to understand what makes things happen when we skate."

I showed them a few basic movements and then made a turn to backwards.

"Now then, boys. Do you know what that turn is called?"

"A twist around?" one of them replied.

"Not a bad try, but that's called a three-turn because my blade makes a print on the ice like a number three.

"What do you do after that?" said Munchy. "A four-turn?"

"No, don't be silly. There's no such thing." I said.

Each one of them tried the turn, and it wasn't long before they got the hang of it.

"You kids learn pretty fast. I'm impressed."

I spent a further enjoyable hour with the kids before saying goodbye.

"I hope I'll see you kids again, soon. Take care."

"Oh, we'll definitely see you again, Charlie." said Speedy. "We want you to be our new coach."

"It's a deal." I said, smiling.

I headed straight into Mr. Johnson's office to tell him the good news.

"There you are, Charlie. You're going to be a big hit around here."

"Well, you know, Mr. Johnson, I was thinking that I'd like to get some classes going, for kids and adults, and get everyone going in the right direction. And we should get some flyers printed, to be posted all over town, and maybe in some neighboring towns, too."

"Sounds good to me, Charlie. I'll get on with it right away."

I left the rink later that day feeling like I finally had something to live for. I was having fun, but I realized it was now time to get down to some serious work if I was ever going to make something of this second chance I'd been given.

The next morning, armed with a bag full of flyers, Billy and I set off around the town, posting flyers on whatever surface we could find. We even stuck one on the ceiling of the barber shop, so when the barber tilted back the chair, the customer would see the flyer, but the local farmer drew the line when he refused to let us stick a flyer on the side of one of his cows.

It's amazing, though, what a little advertising can do. The sleepy town of Warragong Springs was waking up, and waking up fast. Just a few hours after we'd posted the last flyer, the phone started ringing at the ice rink, and never stopped. Ralph Johnson didn't have time to light a cigarette. He and his secretary were booking in one person after another for the classes, and he was quite relieved when I arrived back at the rink.

"Charlie! Am I glad you're back. Take over my phone for a little while, will you? I've just gotta take a break. These classes are going to be a huge success, and it's all thanks to you. Well done, mate!"

With that, Mr. Johnson handed me the phone, and rushed off for a coffee break.

Once the rink had closed, we sat down to work out a schedule for the classes, and divide everyone into age groups. We had about thirty children, and twelve adults, so we figured that we'd have two classes of fifteen children, and one class for all the adults. Billy, to his credit, was quite a good skater, so he would take one children's class, while I took the other. Then, we would both teach the adult class because they needed a little more hand-holding.

By the time I got home that night, I was ready for bed.

We started the classes two days later on a Saturday morning, and everyone was very excited.

"Welcome to the Warragong Springs skating classes!" I proclaimed in a loud voice. A cheer went up.

"If you take a look on the wall, you'll see you names on the list, and which group you're in. Skaters aged eight to fourteen will go to the far end of the rink, skaters under eight years of age will be in the middle section of the rink, and the adults will be at this end of the rink. That way the adults don't have to travel too far to get to their class. Okay, everyone on the ice!"

About thirty kids and twelve adults set foot on the ice for the first time in their lives. As you can imagine, many of the kids were very ambitious, and most of the adults were very careful, but that's human nature.

Before we could get everyone organized the questions started flying.

"How do I move on these things?" "How do I stop?" "How do I go backwards?"

"Backwards?" I replied. "Just be glad if you can go forwards, first!"

A little while later, I heard one kid say to another,

"This is no good. Every step I take to go forwards, I slide three back. How am I going to get to the end of the rink?"

His friend replied, smiling,

"Turn around and skate in the other direction."

All in all, the classes were a big success, and became an enjoyable fixture every Saturday morning. They turned out to be a real money-maker for Ralph Johnson, and he was lavish in his praise for me.

"You've performed a bloody miracle, Charlie. The rink's never had this much money coming in like it has now. At this rate, I'll be able to make a decent settlement with my ex-wife and finally have some peace of mind."

"Oh, I'm sorry." I replied. "I didn't know you'd had any marital problems."

"Oh, yes. And you probably thought you were the only one in this town with problems. My Ex and I never had a smooth passage across the sea of matrimony. There were some bloody big waves, and I capsized frequently!"

A couple of weeks later I was sitting having a cup of coffee, thinking everything was going pretty well. Little did I know that my life was going to take a dramatic turn. For the better or worse? I was about to find out.

10

THE ARRIVAL OF JENNY ATKINS

"Charlie." Mr. Johnson called out, beckoning me into his office. "Take a look at this girl skating 'round the rink. I'm not an expert, but she looks like she knows what she's doing."

I went into his office and looked through the window onto the ice.

"Hey, who is she?" I asked.

"Her name's Jenny Atkins. She and her family just moved into town, so I think I'd better introduce you to them."

"Thanks, Mr. Johnson. She could be a good prospect."

I followed him out of the office, and we walked over to where her parents were sitting.

"Mr. and Mrs. Atkins, this is Charlie Williams. I don't know whether you've heard of him or not, but he's the British Champion, and we're very proud to have him teaching here in our rink."

Mrs. Atkins' mouth dropped open, and Mr. Atkins looked very humble.

"Blimey! This is quite an honor." he said, shifting about on his feet. "I've never met a champion of any sport, before. My name's Bob, and this is my wife, Lucy." Then he reached out to shake hands.

"Nice to meet you both. Wow! You've got a really strong grip, Mr. Atkins."

His wife chimed in.

"Well, he has to, in his line of work. You see, he's a sheep shearer."

"Oh. That explains it." I replied, massaging my hand to get the circulation back into it.

"Yes," joked Mr. Johnson. "Bob's moved here because, for some reason, he couldn't find much work in Melbourne."

We all had a good laugh over that and then Mr. Johnson added,

"And I hear he's a bloody good sheep-shearer, but don't let him talk you into giving you a haircut."

Then Bob turned and called out,

"Jenny!" Come over here and meet your new coach."

Jenny came skating over at top speed and jumped off the ice, nearly knocking me over.

"Oh, my goodness." said her embarrassed mother. "That's a great start, isn't it?"

I just laughed, and said,

"Well, at least I know she's got lots of energy."

"I'm sorry." said a red-faced Jenny. "But I'm pleased to meet you... and I can't wait to have my first lesson with you."

I took an immediate liking to this girl. There was something about her that told me that she would always have the right attitude. And that's a huge plus in this sport.

"Well, if you can't wait for your first lesson, then I'd better get my skates on and check you out right now."

Jenny's face lit up.

'Oh, wow! I'll go and practice some jumps."

While I was lacing up my skates, Bob Atkins came over and sat next to me.

"Er...Charlie. I just thought I'd better say right away that I'm not sure how many lessons I can afford for Jenny. I've only been here a week, and it'll take some time for me to build up my business."

"Don't worry about that right now, Bob. We'll figure out something that works for both of us, but the first lesson I give a skater is always 'on the house' because it's more like a try-out."

"Oh, okay. Thanks, Charlie." he replied. "That's good of you."

I smiled, and went onto the ice. Jenny immediately came over to me.

"Okay, Miss Atkins. Let's see what you're made of. I want to see you skate around the rink, first forwards, and then backwards."

Most of the time, a coach only has to watch a skater take a few strokes to know whether they have a natural feeling, and the coordination, for skating.

I watched Jenny go just once around the rink and was convinced that she had all the right ingredients. Balance, power, a natural alignment over her skate, and a coordination of movement. She was a Ferrari in a rink full of Volkswagens. Not that the Volkswagens wouldn't improve. They just hadn't been skating that long.

I told Jenny's parents that we needed to sit down and make a plan for Jenny's training.

"In that case," Lucy said, "Come over to our place this evening. I'm going to make you a lovely dinner, and then we'll have plenty of time to talk."

"Sounds great to me. Thanks. I'll look forward to it."

That evening, after a home-cooked meal I'd remember for a long time, we sat on their porch and relaxed.

"Well, Bob and Lucy" I said, "I think your daughter has enormous potential. She has a gift that many skaters don't have. Talent. And, right now, she doesn't even know she possesses it, which is actually a good thing because everything she does on the ice is natural, and comes from within her. My job will be to channel this talent in the right direction, and not leave a stone unturned when it comes to teaching her all the aspects of ice skating, but you need to understand, right from the outset, that things don't happen overnight. The championship skaters you see on television have spent years getting to that point, and you've got to be prepared to take the rough with the smooth. I'll coach her to the best of my ability, and your role, as parents, is to be encouraging and supportive. There are going to be days when nothing goes right, and that's when she's going to need you the most. I'll also advise you about equipment, what she should wear, and a hundred other things that you'll need to know."

Bob and Lucy looked at each other, then smiled and nodded their approval.

"Thanks for explaining that, Charlie. Lucy and I know our girl's in the best hands, now, and we're looking forward to a long and, hopefully, successful relationship. Now that we've talked to you, I can see that things weren't exactly organized in the past when she competed. Her previous coach never checked her blades to see if they needed sharpening, never advised on what sort of dress she should wear or how her hair should be worn, and never told her to clean her boots. I can see that things are going to be very different now."

I laid out a basic training plan for Jenny, telling them how many days a week she should skate, and how many hours each day. Then we looked at the calendar and figured out which competitions we should aim for, and what should be our main target for the year.

Jenny could only get to the rink after school - and had to walk nearly two miles to do so - but I planned to teach her every day, Monday through Friday.

"Well, it's been a wonderful evening and I think we've discussed everything we need to for now, so thank you again for a wonderful dinner."

"I'll drive you back to town, Charlie." said Bob.

"Thanks, but you know what? I really want to walk back tonight. I've never seen a sky so clear, and so full of stars."

"But it's nearly three miles..."

"No problem, Bob. It's going to be a pleasure."

11

Moving Onward and, Hopefully, Upward.

∽⌇◞⌇∽

The future looked exciting, but I realized I had a huge responsibility on my hands. It was now up to me to produce some results and thus shape Jenny's future. I could make her, but, unfortunately, I could also break her.

The first day of her new training regimen went better than I could have dreamed. She was enthusiastic, totally fearless, and I could tell immediately that we had a chemistry between us that was going to take us a long way.

"Jenny, that was a great first day, and I'm really pleased with how hard you tried."

"Thank you, Mr. Williams. I'm really looking forward to you being my coach at competitions."

"Me, too, Jenny."

Over the next few weeks she improved beyond all recognition. She had all her double jumps, some combination jumps, and two triple jumps, but her double axel was giving her problems. She wasn't alone. I've seen many skaters get a couple of triple jumps before they perfect their double axel. After all, a double axel is half a revolution more than the other double jumps, which all take off backwards, and it's a forward take-off, which can be quite daunting for some skaters.

A new day dawned, and jenny warmed up in preparation for some serious work on her jumps.

"Jenny, let me see your double axel."

She gathered speed, stepped forward and jumped. Not so good, and I could see what I wanted to work on.

"Okay, Jenny. I want you to realize that a double axel bears little resemblance to a single axel. I don't want to get too scientific here, but do you remember I told you about the 'Parabola', which is the curve of your travel from the take-off, up to the top of a jump, and then down to the landing? Well, on a single axel you can jump up and then rotate at the top of that Parabola, but unless you can jump really high, the rotation for a double axel needs to start on the way up because you're only in the air for the same amount of time as a single axel, and yet you've got to complete one more revolution. So I want you to 'snap' your take-off more and then quickly switch to your 'air position' with your legs squeezed tightly together, just as you would if you wanted to rotate quickly in a back spin. If your free leg is loose, and far away from the leg you're going to land on, you just won't rotate quickly enough. Okay, lecture over, so let's give it another try. Don't use a lot of energy stepping forward to jump. Take care how you step forward into the right position and then use your energy to jump."

Jenny understood and skated around the rink to set up the jump.

"Now, hold your free foot back until you're going to spring up on your skating knee." I yelled. "Then lift it through quickly."

She stepped forward onto a well-bent knee and then sprung up into the air better than ever before. Then a nice tight air position gave her the best chance of completing the revolutions so that she could land backwards without a 'cheated' turn on the landing.

"Attagirl, Jenny! That's the way to do it."

"Wow!" she exclaimed. "Everything happens so quickly."

"Yes. Because you're only in the air for half a second, or maybe six or seven tenths, and everything has to take place in that time. A top-level male skater jumping a triple axel is in the air for about one second, but that's it, no longer."

"Okay Mr. Williams, I've got it now." said Jenny, with a big smile.

I smiled to myself as she skated off to practice some more jumps, and realized now that I had a lot to live for. I not only had a nice place in which to earn a regular income, but an exciting prospect to work with. And I had to admire the toughness of this girl. She walked nearly two miles to the rink every day from her school near the sheep-shearing station, in the hot Australian sunshine, and never complained.

I taught a lot of lessons during the rest of the day, and wasn't too sorry when the Zamboni came out to resurface the ice at the end of the last freestyle session. I'd done a good day's work and was thirsty, so I headed to the Crazy Kangaroo Bar.

"Hi Billy, a nice cold Pepsi please."

"Yeah, very funny, Charlie."

"No, I mean it."

"You really don't want your usual beer?"

"No. I don't need it, and I really want to have a clear head in the morning coaching Jenny, so drink it yourself."

"Blimey, mate," replied Billy, "You really are serious!"

"Yes, Billy. That's one of the glorious things about life. It sometimes gives you a second chance, and I think I'd better grab it with both hands."

I finished my Pepsi, but didn't feel like going back to my lodging right away, so I called the local cinema.

"Is that the Carlton Cinema? What time does the film start this evening?"

"Well, what time can you get here." said the voice on the other end.

"Are you serious?" I replied.

"Yeah. This is a small town, and you'll very likely be our only customer tonight."

And you know something? I was.

The next day Jenny arrived later than usual. She was wearing shorts and a T-shirt so I couldn't help seeing all the cuts and grazes on her legs. She also had a nasty black eye.

"Have you been in a car crash, or something?" I asked.

"Oh, the cuts and grazes? That's because I like to climb trees."

"And how did you get that black eye?" I asked.

"I got into a fight at school this morning."

"Well, it looks like you got the worst of it." I said.

She tried to hold back a smile, but couldn't.

"Not really, Mr. Williams. You should see the other girl."

I shook my head in disbelief. How, I thought to myself, am I ever going to get this girl to have the grace of a ballerina?

"Well, you don't have to look beautiful today, so get your skating clothes on and let's get to work. You've got a big competition coming up in three weeks."

I had set out Jenny's daily training program in much the same way I had trained. A five day week, with the weekends off, unless we really needed to cram an extra couple of hours in on a Saturday or Sunday, when it got closer to a competition.

I think it's good for a skater, and indeed any athlete, to have at least one day a week away from their sport, so that when they start the new week they'll feel refreshed and look forward to training. They will also have given themselves a break, physically, and more importantly, mentally. I've known some young skaters who skate seven days a week, but I don't know whether they do it because they want to, or because their parents think they need to put in that much time. If it's the skater's choice, and they enjoy it, then there's no harm, but they do run the risk of 'burning out' by the time they become teenagers. Skating should never seem like a job, and if you're not looking forward to going to the rink it's going to show in your skating. Skating is hard enough, but if your not enthusiastic about it, you're never going to do well.

My skaters' programs were choreographed by a new young coach who had arrived at the rink a week before I did. She did a great job of molding Jenny into an artistic, fluid skater, and I really liked the program she choreographed.

Each day's training would start with off-ice stretching and limbering up before the skaters put on their skates. This would get them ready for the demands skating puts on their bodies. Then, it's onto the ice for some basic 'stroking', forwards and backwards, on strong edges.

There are so many different exercises skaters can do on the ice, so I tell my skaters to vary them each day so that they don't do exactly the same on-ice warm up routine every day.

At the end of this particular day, I told my skaters to meet me in the snack area once they'd taken off their skates.

"Okay, skaters, I'm not going to keep you long, but I wanted to talk about nervousness, and how to handle it. Now, some of you may not feel any nerves when you compete, and that's great. But most skaters feel a little anxiety when they're going to skate in a competition, and that's quite normal. You're only human, and you might be worried that you're not going to do as well as expected."

One of my youngest skaters put up her hand.

"Sometimes, I forget my program when I skate in a competition."

"Well, that's usually because your mind is being distracted, and there could be several reasons for that. Performing in front of a panel of judges, skating in a different ice rink, or being distracted by the cheering of the audience. These are just some of the things that could make you forget your program or feel nervous, because everything feels so different to your usual daily routine where you're comfortable in your surroundings. So the best advice is to practice your program again and again until it becomes almost automatic. Then, you can concentrate on how you perform it. Just tell yourself that you've skated your program many, many times in practice, and all you've got to do is go out there and do it one more time.

And here is one final bit of advice that I found very effective. If you feel those 'butterflies' in your stomach - that nasty fluttery feeling - there is a very useful exercise that should get rid of them. Breath in deeply, completely filling your lungs, and then exhale through a very tiny hole between your lips, ensuring that it will take about ten seconds to exhale completely. Controlling the exhale through that tiny hole in your lips should make the muscles around your stomach feel much calmer and steadier. You can repeat this once or twice more, but don't hyperventilate."

A few days later I was sitting in the rink having a cup of coffee and a doughnut when a large Mercedes-Benz pulled up outside. The driver got out and walked around to open the rear passenger door. A young girl and a woman got out.

"Thank you, Merryman." said the woman. "Come back for us at precisely six p.m."

"Yes, ma'am." replied Merryman, touching his cap.

Considering they were just visiting an ice rink, I thought they were quite fashionably dressed.

They came in and saw me sitting there.

"Can you please tell me where I can find Mr. Charles Williams?"

"You've already found him. That's me."

"Oh. You're a lot younger than I anticipated, but that doesn't matter. All that's important is your reputation and expertise."

"Thank you. You flatter me."

"I'm Helen Forbes-Cunningham and this is my daughter, Fiona. You've probably heard of her."

"No, I'm afraid I haven't, but I haven't been here very long, so forgive me."

"Say hello to Mr. Williams, Fiona."

"Good afternoon, Mr. Williams." said Fiona, putting on the sweetest of smiles.

"Well, I'll get straight to the point, Charles. I want you to take over the training of my daughter. She's already a successful skater and, of course, her immediate ambition is to be Australian champion."

"Well." I replied, "I like ambitious skaters, and I'll be happy to do everything I can to help her achieve her goal."

"That's what I want to hear." said a satisfied Helen Forbes-Cunningham. "We'll want a lesson every day, and more if necessary. Money is no problem, so, whatever it takes. Fiona auditioned successfully for 'The Australian Ballet School', so you'll see an obvious grace in her skating."

"I can't wait to see her skate." I said. "Can we start now? There's still an hour left on this freestyle session."

"Oh, can I, mummy?" said an excited Fiona. "I'd like to show Mr. Williams what I can do."

"Of course, my dear. It's just as well you brought your skates in with you. Go and get changed."

While Fiona was changing, we sat down and I had another coffee. Helen Forbes-Cunningham ordered tea.

"As we have rather a long family name, it will be quite alright if you call me Helen."

"Thank you...Helen."

I didn't know it at the time, but I was about to step into fairly deep waters. I had a gut feeling that, in Fiona, I was going to be dealing with a piece of fine china, but then I told myself I shouldn't be too hasty in my judgment.

This was going to be interesting. I now had two skaters from very different backgrounds training alongside each other. One has to walk two miles to the rink in the heat of the day, the other arrives in an air-conditioned Mercedes-Benz.

Helen put her cup down and looked me square in the eye.

"Charles, I want you to realize that I expect Fiona to win the championship. I leave no stone unturned when it comes to ensuring success. I wanted wealth, so I married a very successful businessman. And I want success for my daughter, so I've put her with the best coaches, choreographers, and fitness trainers that I can find. I always get what I want."

"Well, I admire your determination, Helen. I have to say, though, that there are no guarantees in this sport, but I'll do my part to the best of my ability, so we'll let the chips fall where they may."

"They need to fall in my direction, Charles."

"Alright, Helen." I replied. "I think I'd better get on the ice."

Fiona got on the ice shortly afterwards, and I gave her some time to warm up. Then I called Jenny over to meet her.

"Jenny, I want you to meet Fiona. You've probably seen each other at competitions, but you may not have been introduced."

"Hi Fiona!" said Jenny, shaking Fiona's hand vigorously. "Yes, we've seen each other at competitions."

"Hello, Jenny." replied Fiona, politely.

"Now, girls." I said. "Even though you're in direct competition with each other I want you to get on well together, and support each other, too. This will be a great training environment for both of you."

"I think it's great that you're going to be here, Fiona." said Jenny, eagerly. "You'll have to come over to my place and climb some trees with me."

"Oh my goodness, no." replied a shocked Fiona.

"Oh, well. Please yourself. You don't know what you're missing."

I intervened quickly.

"Okay, Jenny, I'll see you later. Fiona's going to have her first lesson with me now."

It didn't take me long to see that Fiona had a very nice quality about her skating. Her ballet training had served her well, and she always looked in perfect alignment over her skate. Her jumps were not dynamic, but well-controlled, and her spins were well-centered in beautiful positions. I counted myself lucky that I had two very nice skaters working towards the championships, and I had to be careful not to play favorites.

"Well, Fiona, you skate very nicely, so I'll map out a plan with your mother to make sure that you come up to the championships in good order."

"Thank you, Mr. Williams. I know I'm going to enjoy training with you."

That evening, I thought it was time to get a letter off to my parents.

> *Dear Mum and Dad,*
>
> *How are you both? I hope all is well with you.*
>
> *I apologize that it's been a while since I last wrote, but there has been so much going on here. I now have two nice prospects for the Australian championships, and the classes I started at the rink have been a great success. Mr. Johnson is very pleased with me, and we get on really well together. He's like so many of the people I've met here in Australia - friendly, helpful, and positive. He has a great outlook on life and is very encouraging. So far, I'm very impressed with this country.*

As for the bangers and mash, mum, keep 'em warm, because I'll plan on a trip back to England after the championships. On second thoughts, give them to dad. I'll want some fresh ones when I come home!

I haven't been able to keep up with any news from England because we are rather out in the 'boonies' here, so what's been happening? Has all the fuss died down about Jimmy? What length of ban did they end up giving him? And who's training him now? Have any more bad things been said about me? I hope there are still some people who believe in me, and that I didn't look like a guilty person who was running away. I know one day all this mess will be resolved, but until then I've got to survive, and so far I'm proud to say I think I'm doing it pretty well. And I'm sure a lot of it is down to the two of you. I've got a little of your common sense, mum, and a bit of dad's toughness, too. So you needn't worry about me. I'll be okay!

I'll try to write more often, so until then,

All my love,
Charlie.

I mailed the letter the next day, but not before I gave it a quick kiss before dropping it into the mail box. I wonder if other people do that when they're mailing a letter to someone special?

12

A LOT HAPPENING

With just one week left before the Victoria Trophy competition in Melbourne, both girls were training up a storm. As soon as Jenny landed a triple jump, Fiona would skate off and do the same. There was definitely a tension in the air when these girls were on the ice at the same time, but I didn't feel that it was causing any problems so I let them get on with it.

I experienced the same thing when I was training back in London. Five days a week I would see my main rivals working hard, and that was all the incentive I needed to spur me on to be better than them. Competition definitely improves the breed.

The next morning was a morning I'd remember for a long time.

"Isn't today April Fool's Day?" Jenny said, as I went to get on the ice.

"Yes, I think it is." I replied. "Why, what mischief are you up to?"

"Oh, nothing." she said, with a very impish look on her face. I was about to find out that it was far from nothing.

I stepped onto the ice and immediately felt something was wrong. For a prank, Jenny had put clear nail varnish on the running edges of my blades, and they immediately slipped out from under me, causing me to fall heavily. The mug of coffee I was carrying spilled all over the ice and it made me very angry.

"You little idiot! Look what you've done!"

Realizing that she had done something stupid, she rushed off the ice and ran straight into the ladies rest room, crying uncontrollably. I got up and went off the ice to sit down. I was really mad at her, but after a few minutes I calmed down and waited for her to come out. Eventually she did. I grabbed her hand and sat her down in a quiet corner of the rink.

"Jenny, you need to understand that I got angry because I could have really hurt myself as a result of your stupid prank. That was a very childish thing to do, and I'm going to have to think about whether I should continue teaching you."

Jenny was still sobbing as she tried to get some words out.

"I'm sorry Mr. Williams." she said, sobbing between her words, "Really I am. I'll never do anything so stupid again."

"What makes me really mad, Jenny, is that you have something very special that can't be taught, but you're almost throwing it away by playing a prank like that."

She sat there with her head bowed, staring at the ground, and then I saw a transformation in her character taking place right before me.

She lifted her head up a little and said,

"If you'll please keep teaching me, Mr. Williams, you'll find I'm going to be a different person from now on. I guess it's time for me to grow up and show a little maturity."

I looked at her for a while and found that I just couldn't stay angry, because I knew those words came from her heart, so I put my arm around her shoulder and gave her a hug. She rested her head on my shoulder and started sobbing again, but this time from relief.

They say that every cloud has a silver lining, and in the long run this little episode may well have been a blessing in disguise, teaching Jenny one of life's important lessons that would stand her in good stead for the rest of her life.

In the days leading up to the competition I saw a different Jenny Atkins. She had grown up in the space of a week, and although she was always very determined, she now showed a new maturity in her manner, and didn't let her emotions get the better of her.

The Victoria Trophy was on Saturday, but we decided to drive to Melbourne on Thursday and have an easy day on Friday with just one practice. Then there would be a final practice on the Saturday morning, and the competition in the afternoon. Bob had to stay and work, so I went in the car with Jenny and her mother.

"It seems like you have to get used to driving long distances here in Australia, Lucy." I said.

"Yes, and especially as we live in Warragong Springs. Everywhere we go is a long drive, but we get used to it. So, today, we'll drive about three hours and then stop for lunch."

"Sounds good to me." I replied.

Lucy was a very good driver, so I reclined my seat a little, closed my eyes, and began to wonder what was happening back in England. I wasn't to know it at the time, but as it turns out there was quite a lot happening...

Although Jimmy Donovan had been banned from competing for a year, he was still quite young and had several good years ahead of him, so he had started training with a new coach, Arthur Begley. Arthur is another one of those old-time coaches who's seen it all. If anyone could handle Jimmy, he could. Everything went fairly smoothly for a while, but things were getting ugly in the Donovan household.

From what people had told me, Jimmy had never had much of a life, but ever since the inquiry his life had become a living hell. Every day, his father would berate him over one thing or another.

"My God! I'm ashamed and embarrassed that you're my son." moaned his father. "You can't do anything right. And now you've got a one year ban from competing." He turned to his wife.

"Go into the other room, Sandra. Obviously, our son hasn't learned his lesson."

"George, please don't hurt him." she pleaded.

"Go into the other room, I said!"

Reluctantly, his wife obeyed orders, and quietly left the room.

Jimmy's father unbuckled his belt and took it off. Jimmy looked terrified.

"No, dad...please, No!"

He then folded the belt to double it's thickness and proceeded to thrash Jimmy on every part of his body.

"Ow! No, please stop, dad." Jimmy screamed.

"Ow!...Ow!"

Jimmy was defenseless, and the pain from each blow he received made him yell louder and louder. This relentless punishment went on for about two minutes, and then his father smacked the side of his head so hard that he fell to the floor, crying uncontrollably.

"Let that be a lesson to you, you useless little piece of rubbish. You're not *my* son!" And with that, his father stormed out of the room.

It would be impossible to know just what would have been going through Jimmy's mind at that time. The pain, the suffering, and the torment, must have been unbearable. And the despair. Probably wondering if there was anything left worth living for. You wouldn't have blamed the boy if he'd considered suicide might be the easy way out at that moment. And, sadly, his mother was too scared to show him any sympathy in front of his father.

Then, just five days later...

"I thought I told you to clean your room, Jimmy." said his father, angrily. "But you don't listen, do you?" He started to unbuckle his belt again, and Jimmy felt the blood starting to race through his veins. His father smacked him in the face a couple of times, and at that moment Jimmy thought to himself...no more, not this time! Knowing he had nothing to lose, he quickly grabbed a kitchen chair and swung it at his father, sending him crashing to the floor. A look of shock, and total disbelief, registered on his father's face as Jimmy picked up the chair again.

"No, Jimmy, please...don't!" cried his father as he curled up into a ball, trying to protect himself. "I'm your father!"

Jimmy felt himself getting into an uncontrollable rage. He screamed out,

"You said I'm not your son! So that means you can't be my father. Now, see how you like this!"

Jimmy dealt his father another heavy blow to the head with the chair, rendering him unconscious. His mother came running into the room.

"Oh, my God, what have you done, Jimmy?"

"I couldn't help it, mum." he cried. "He was going to give me another beating, and I can't take the pain any more."

"Alright, Jimmy. I'd better call for an ambulance quickly."

He put down the chair and tried to get his thoughts together. After she got off the phone she put her arms around him, and tried to ease his pain.

"Try to calm down, Jimmy. Everything's going to be okay."

"Why has he hated me all these years, mum? What have I done wrong?"

"It's not you, Jimmy, but I'm afraid he's a sick man. For years, now, he feels that life has been cruel and unkind to him, and a horrible anger has been building up inside him. When you were younger he had a good job and had high hopes of promotion to a better position in the company, but they gave that position to a younger man, and that's when the bitterness started to show in his character."

Jimmy looked down at his father's lifeless body.

"He's not moving, mum. I'm going to the Police station to tell them I've probably killed my father. I'll tell them everything, and tell them that I'll take what's coming to me."

"No, Jimmy, don't do that. I can see he's breathing, so he's probably just unconscious. but don't say anything about this to anyone. I'll have to go to the hospital with him, and I'll call you as soon as I know how he is."

The next day Jimmy went into the rink with a black eye, and bruises on his face.

"What happened to you, Jimmy?" asked Mr. Begley.

"Oh...I fell off my bicycle yesterday."

"No you didn't." replied Mr. Begley, abruptly. "Your dad's hit you again, hasn't he?"

"No, no, he didn't."

Arthur was a died-in-the-wool Yorkshireman who stood no nonsense.

"I'm going to call the authorities." he said, bluntly. "Don't you worry, lad, there's not going to be any more of this. And don't bother to put on your skates because we may have to go somewhere."

With that, he stormed off into the manager's office. A few minutes later he came out and called Jimmy over.

"Listen, lad. I know this is not going to be easy for you, but the police are going to be here soon, and it's important that you tell them the truth about what's been going on. You've done nothing wrong, lad, but it's now becoming common knowledge that your dad's been abusing you. This can't go on any longer."

Jimmy looked vacant for a few seconds, and then suddenly broke down.

"Sit down Jimmy, and let it all out."

When he had stopped crying, Jimmy realized that he could no longer keep his fears to himself.

"Oh, Mr. Begley, I fought back against my dad yesterday and he ended up in hospital, but my mum said he'll be out very soon so I'm scared, and I don't know which way to turn. I can't take this any more. And whenever my mother tries to stand up to him, he'll hit her, too. I think there's something wrong with him."

Looking very despondent, Jimmy continued.

"All my friends have fathers who love them, and encourage them, and that's all I wanted from my dad. Just for him to be a real dad. It's not much to ask, is it? But now I realize I'll never have a father like that."

Arthur put his hand on Jimmy's shoulder and said,

"You're a brave lad, Jimmy. We'll get this sorted out one way or another."

Twenty minutes later the police arrived, and the manager invited them into his office along with Jimmy and Arthur Begley. The manager spoke first.

"Good morning, officers. I'm John Hillman, the manager of this ice rink, and this is Arthur Begley, our head coach."

"Good morning, sir. I'm Chief Inspector Carpenter, and this is Sergeant Briggs."

After a lot of formal handshaking, they all sat down.

"Now, then." said the Chief Inspector, "You must be Jimmy Donovan."

"Yes, sir." replied Jimmy, looking quite scared.

"Well, Jimmy, that's quite a shiner you've got, there, but I need to ask you a few questions, so I want you to relax and tell me as much as you can about what's been going on."

Once Jimmy realized that the officers were on his side, he did relax, and proceeded to tell the Chief Inspector almost everything that had happened to him. When he'd finished, the Chief Inspector, who had probably dealt with hundreds of domestic abuse cases, looked quite shocked.

"My goodness! You *have* been through the mill."

Jimmy nodded.

"When I was a young kid, he was a great father, and we had lots of fun, but..." His voice trailed away.

"That's the problem, Jimmy." said a consoling Chief Inspector. "People change. And it's sometimes very hard to find out why. Although, in this case, it's pretty obvious that he became a very bitter man after he was turned down for that new position in his work. I'm glad you told me about that because it helps us understand the man."

"Well, sir, when things started getting bad he used to just yell at me, but then he started hitting me, and my life has become a nightmare."

"Well, I wouldn't expect you to know this, Jimmy," explained the Chief Inspector, "But one in five children in this country have been exposed to domestic violence."

"No, I didn't know that." replied Jimmy.

"And I'm sorry to have to tell you this, Jimmy, but your father is going to be picked up for questioning and held on suspicion of domestic violence, and if there is enough evidence against him he will be charged with that offence, along with 'Grievous Bodily Harm'."

Jimmy sat quietly with his head bowed, and, once again, you wonder what must have been going through his head at that moment.

"Jimmy," said the Chief Inspector, 'Would you mind waiting outside for a minute?"

"Certainly, sir."

After he had gone out of the room the Chief Inspector addressed John Hillman and Arthur Begley.

"You're going to have to keep a watchful eye on Jimmy. Children exposed to domestic violence are more likely to have behavioral and emotional problems. He seems a bit of a sensitive boy, and this could end up tragically if we're not careful."

After several weeks of investigation and inquiries George Frederick Donovan finally ended up in court. The proceedings were long and complex. At one point in the trial the judge turned to Jimmy's dad and asked,

"Mr. Donovan, do you have anything you wish to say in your defense?"

"Yes, your Honor, I do. I regret my actions, but when I failed in my job I decided that Jimmy was not going to suffer the same fate, and that I was going to make sure that he was perfect in everything he did. Failure was not going to be an option, and if he faltered in any way, he'd have to answer to me."

"A very high-handed attitude I must say, Mr. Donovan." remarked the judge.

"I realize that, now, your Honor."

At the end of the trial the judge summed up by saying that George Donovan had mercilessly beaten his defenseless son on more than one occasion, and would have to pay his debt to society. The only mitigating circumstances were that he had no previous convictions, and showed great remorse. When the trial was eventually over, and the smoke cleared, he was handed down a sentence of four years in prison, with a possible reduction for good behavior.

13

Down to Business

Meanwhile, back down under on an Australian freeway, three hours went by fairly quickly, and Lucy pulled off the road into one of the many transport cafes along the route.

"This is a good one because a lot of truckers stop here, so you know the food is good." she said.

"That's just what we look for in England, too." I replied. "It's not five-star food, but clean, nutritious, and satisfying. So, Lucy, do you think they'll have a plate of lettuce here for our budding champion?"

"Aw, come on Mr. Williams." moaned Jenny. "I've got to have more than that. I'm pretty light, right now."

"Yes, of course, Jenny." I replied. "I was just teasing you. You can have a decent meal."

And we did have a very decent meal before getting back on the road again.

Three and a half hours later we arrived at the hotel, and when we checked in they told me that there was a message for me to call my mother and father. It said they had some good news for me, so as soon as I got into my room I picked up the phone.

"Hello, dad?" I said. "What's happened?"

"Well, Charlie," replied dad. "The skating world's buzzing with the news, so I wanted you to know that Jimmy was interviewed by the police, and the long and short of it is that his father has been sent to prison for four years on an abuse charge, so things are starting to straighten out. And Arthur Begley and Miss Cook send you their regards. I think everyone here knows you're innocent, but until Jimmy admits that he lied, everything's still up in the air."

"Oh, that's great, dad." I replied, feeling very relieved. "So there's hope, yet."

We chatted for a couple of minutes more before saying our goodbyes. After I put down the phone I thought for a moment and then picked it up again.

"Hello, Lucy?"

"Yes, Charlie. What is it?"

"Well, I just thought that as we've been sitting in the car for all these hours, we should go out and stretch our legs and get some fresh air."

"Good idea, Charlie. How about we see you down in the lobby in about ten minutes?"

"Perfect. See you down there."

We had a nice walk for about thirty minutes and then headed back to the hotel for an early dinner and a good night's sleep.

The day of the competition dawned and both girls had a very good final practice.

"Okay, girls. You've both worked really well up to this competition and there's no doubt that you're ready. All you're going out there to do is what you've done a hundred or more times before, so that should make you feel very confident. It's one more time, but with a bit more performance quality if you can. From what I understand, we need to do well in these open competitions to have a good chance in the State

Championships, so you've really got to go for it. Now, it's about five hours to the competition, so let's get back to the hotel so that you can have a light snack. You should never eat within two or three hours of a competition because your lungs won't be able to expand if your stomach is too full."

The girls had a nutritious snack, and three hours later we were back at the arena going through the usual warm-up routine, followed by the ritual of applying make-up, doing the hair, and all the other things that give me an excuse to take a coffee break.

Before we knew it, it was time for the girls to lace up their boots and check in with the ice monitor to make sure he knew that both my skaters were present.

We stood around waiting for the announcement for the skaters to get on the ice for their warm-up. If a skater is going to feel a little nervous, this is when it usually happens. You just want to get out there and get on with it.

"Will the first five skaters please take the ice for a five-minute warm-up." a voice said over the loudspeakers.

Jenny had drawn in the first group, Fiona in the second, so I was glad that I could concentrate on each one individually. I had to admit to myself that I felt a little nervous because once the skater goes out there to skate their program, there's nothing more you can do as a coach. It's out of your hands now, and you can feel quite helpless. That's why I trained to be one hundred and one percent ready as a skater, and train my skaters to be the same.

The warm-up went well and Jenny looked confident. She had drawn third to skate, which was ideal. Just enough time to get her breath back, have a sip of water, blow her nose, and get her thoughts together to remember the most important things.

"That was a good warm-up, Jenny. Just keep the same timing into your jumps, and pace yourself. You get a good breather in the slow section, so you'll be able to finish strongly."

"I hope I make mum and dad proud of me." she replied.

"You will, Jenny. You will." I said, smiling.

I could see Fiona pacing up and down in a passage nearby, and hoped she wasn't working herself up too much.

In no time at all the announcer proclaimed,

"And now, representing the Skating Club of Warragong Springs, please welcome Jenny Atkins!"

There was a big round of applause and Jenny skated out to the center of the ice as though she owned the place, acknowledging the audience.

Jenny skated flawlessly, and received a huge ovation. When she came off the ice I gave her a big hug and hearty congratulations. Considering that she skated early in the event her marks were very satisfactory.

"You did it! That was a great skate!" I said, excitedly.

"Oh, thanks Mr. Williams. You gave me such confidence, so I knew I could do it all."

"Okay. I'm so proud of you, but I've got to be with Fiona now. She's in the next warm-up in a couple of minutes. I'll see you and your mum and dad later."

"Fiona. Are you all set for the warm-up?"

"Yes, Mr. Williams, I'm ready. Is my mother upstairs watching?"

"Well...yes, I think so. I'm sure she'll want to watch you skate. Don't you want her to?"

"Er...yes. If I skate well."

"Fiona. Don't even worry about your mother. What's important is you. You don't need to feel any extra pressure. You've worked hard for this moment, and I'm looking forward to watching you skate like I know you can. You're very special, and I know your mother's proud of you."

Those words seemed to relax her, and she even cracked a little smile.

"That's my girl. Let's have a good warm-up now, but remember we planned for you to come off the ice a minute before the end of it because you're the first to skate in this group."

Fiona's warm-up went well, too, and she came off the ice for a quick breather.

"Okay. You're skating beautifully, so just get your breath back and you're ready to go."

When it was Fiona's turn to skate out onto the ice, she, too, received a warm round of applause. Her program was a joy to watch, and she made no mistakes. Artistically, she was superior to Jenny, but technically Jenny had more speed and elevation on her jumps. It was going to be a close run thing, and I would have been happy to see a tie between them.

There were twelve skaters in the event and some of them were pretty good, but I really felt that my two girls should be first and second. They were just that much better than the rest.

After the last girl had skated we figured it would be another twenty or thirty minutes before they posted the results, so we found a place to sit down and relax for a while. It was actually forty-five minutes before we saw a lady walking towards us with some papers in her hand. Then she went over to a wall and taped the results onto it. Everyone surged forward to see them and eventually we got close enough to see for ourselves. There it was. First: Jennifer Atkins, Second: Fiona Forbes-Cunningham. A great result for Jenny, and me, but it created a bit of an awkward situation. I gave Jenny a congratulatory hug, but it was clear from the look on Fiona's face that she was very disappointed, and must have thought that she should have won. I put my arm around her shoulder and tried to console her with some encouraging remarks.

"You couldn't have skated better, and you can see how close the marks are between first and second. It could have gone either way."

"Yes, but it didn't, did it?" said a voice behind me.

I turned around to see a stone-faced Helen Forbes-Cunningham looking quite disgusted.

"Helen. There's no telling how the judging is going to come out. That's why we have seven judges here, and it will be nine at Nationals. This result was a four-three split, and with one different judge on the panel it could well have been a four-three split in Fiona's favor. Try to see the positive side of things, and let's work towards the next competition in a good frame of mind."

She thought for a moment, and then said,

"Alright, Charles. I think we can do that. We'll be leaving right after the podium ceremony today, but Fiona will be at the rink on Monday for her lesson at the usual time. Thank you."

"Thank you, Helen."

It was obvious that, for the time leading up to the championships, there was going to be a certain amount of tension in our rink, and that was putting it mildly. There were more competitions ahead of us, leading up to the National Championship, and I could already see that I was not only going to have to be a coach, but a referee as well.

Monday came soon enough, and before I took each one of them for their lesson I called them over for a quick talk.

"Okay, girls, you both skated very well on Saturday, and I couldn't be more pleased with you but, as athletes, there are certain things you must keep in mind.

When we compete we are mentally gearing ourselves up for the big moment, and then we give it our all. So, naturally, after a big performance there is often, what we call, a let-down period where you sometimes unwind so much that you feel 'flat'. And if you were going to experience that, it would probably be now, a day or two after the event. So if you feel a bit low on energy today, don't let it worry you. It's perfectly normal. It's a bit of an emotional roller coaster getting yourselves 'up' for an event, and then relaxing afterwards only to find that you have to build yourself up again a couple of weeks later. So this could have happened to you both this past weekend, and it's just one example of how you have to get yourself in the right frame of mind after a competition. It's so important to consider the mental aspect of this sport. You can be as fit as a fiddle, and as strong as an ox, but if your mind is all over the place and you can't concentrate, you could 'blow it', big time."

The girls didn't say anything, but nodded their heads.

"Okay. Let's get to work. Fiona, you've got to try and make your jumps bigger, and Jenny, you've got to work on your artistry and get a bit more emotion and feeling into your skating."

Each girl had her strong points, and it was going to be interesting to see which one would improve on their weak points to become the 'complete' skater. Hopefully, they both would. As for the parents, they were as different as chalk and cheese. I felt so comfortable with Jenny's mother and father. They were friendly and down to earth, and had complete trust in me, but Fiona's mother didn't make it easy for me to feel the same way about her because of her cold, business-like attitude. Then again, she may have felt that she needed to be that way in order to make her intentions, and expectations, perfectly clear. I hadn't met her husband because it was my understanding that he was always away on business trips, but I often wondered what sort of a man he was.

There was one more competition before the State Championships, and that was the Canberra Open. Once again, both girls skated very well, finishing first and second, but this time Fiona came out on top.

"Congratulations, Fiona!" said Jenny, shaking Fiona's hand on the podium.

"Thank you." replied Fiona, uneasily.

I was happy to see that gracious gesture from Jenny. And it was quite genuine, too. I was also happy to see a slight smile on Helen's face. The first one I'd seen since the day I met her.

"There you are, Helen. This time Fiona deserved to win, and that's how it turned out."

"Yes. She was clearly the best, wasn't she? Let's hope this continues."

14

There's Always a Hiccup

~⁓◯⁓~

With less than four weeks to the State Championships I wanted everything to run as smoothly as possible for all concerned, but trouble reared it's ugly head yet again. Jenny seemed unusually quiet during her lesson, so when it was over I said,

"Jenny. Is anything wrong? I don't think I've ever known you to be so quiet."

"I'm sorry. I don't want to talk about it, Mr. Williams."

"Now look, Jenny, we can't go on like this. Something's happened. What is it?"

"Well, someone anonymously sent my mum and dad an English newspaper that had an article about you in it. And it was really bad. It said you'd done something really dishonest and were banned from teaching in Great Britain."

"Oh my God. Jenny, I think you need to know the truth about this, so take off your skates and come with me to Mr. Johnson's office."

We sat down in his office and I explained what had happened.

"Mr. Johnson, I can only think that, with the championships not too far away, this has been done to psyche out both Jenny and myself. It's a dirty ploy and I'm pretty sure who's behind it."

Then I turned to Jenny and gave her a brief history of what had happened in England. I concluded by saying,

"Jenny, you have to believe that I never gave Jimmy Donovan a drug. I hate anything to do with drugs, but he had to say that in order to transfer the blame to me because he knew his father would beat him if he thought he had taken drugs on his own. The problem was, the skating association and the press believed him, so that finished me as a coach. I had to leave England, but I swear on my mother's and father's lives that I'm innocent."

Then Ralph Johnson spoke up.

"Jenny, I believe Charlie is completely innocent, otherwise I would never have employed him here at the rink. I'm sure the truth will come out sometime in the future, but until then we have to believe in Charlie. And, clearly, this has definitely been done at this time to make you lose faith in him, and even turn you against him. I'm afraid it doesn't take much figuring out who would benefit if you were brought down mentally and had the stuffing knocked out of you."

"Yes. I see what you mean, Mr. Johnson." said Jenny, looking very relieved. "It has to be that bi..., well, I'd better not used that word. I'm supposed to be growing up to be a lady."

Ralph Johnson laughed, and said,

"So, are you two still a team?"

"You bet!" replied Jenny, as she came over to give me a big hug. "I always did think he had an honest face."

I felt greatly relieved.

"Thanks for seeing us, Mr. Johnson. It's a pity this sort of thing has to happen, but there obviously seems to be a lot at stake. I think I'd better call Jenny's parents and let them know exactly what we've talked about this morning. And, Jenny, try not act any differently toward Fiona. I think she's an innocent party in a very nasty business, but if she does know anything about this, let her wonder."

That evening I went over to see Jenny's parents, and once again her mother made me a lovely dinner. As we ate, I reiterated what I'd said to Jenny in Ralph Johnson's office and Bob and Lucy couldn't have been more gracious. Bob spoke first.

"Charlie, if you say you didn't do it, then that's fine with us. We'll stand by you all the way. We believe in you, and after all you've done for our Jenny, that's the least we could do. We think you're a bloody marvel."

"Thanks for that vote of confidence, Bob. It's good to know there are people who believe in me, but enough of that. How's the sheep shearing business going? I'd like to come and watch you some day."

"Getting better every week, I'm happy to say. And don't think Jenny is the only competitor in this family. I'm in a sheep-shearing contest in a couple of weeks right here on the station. You might be able to get some good odds on me with the bookmakers because I'm not known in this area."

"Oh, great!" I said. "If I'm free I'll definitely be there."

"And did you know, Charlie, that there's a World Machine Shearing championship? The record for shearing a sheep is about forty-five seconds, but I'm not in that league. This competition's just a local one, mainly for fun."

"And what about you, Lucy? Are you competitive in any way?" I asked.

Lucy just shrugged her shoulders and replied,

"Well, sometimes I have to get Bob's dinner ready in record time, if that counts?"

"Mum's dinners are the best, aren't they, Mr. Williams?" said Jenny, enthusiastically.

"I can certainly vouch for that, Jenny. If I wasn't keeping fit skating every day I could put on a lot of weight in this house."

As Lucy was clearing away the dishes I thought to myself, what a happy household this is. And it was, but there were clouds forming on the horizon.

Two days later Bob came home from the station looking very glum.

"What is it, Bob? What's the matter?" said a concerned Lucy.

"Well, we've got a new foreman at the station, and he's coming down heavy on me. This afternoon he told me that I'm not shearing enough sheep each hour, and that if I don't speed up my work, he's going to have to let me go. The thing is, the previous foreman was quite happy with the number of sheep I sheared each hour, and I do more each hour than my mates, so I feel like I'm being victimized."

Lucy took Bob's hand and gave it a squeeze.

"Can you work any faster?"

"Not really, Lucy. I'm working about as fast as I can now. But I've got a nasty feeling that there's more to this than meets the eye. You see, when I said I'd like to speak to the boss of the station, the foreman said, 'No chance, mate. Mr. Forbes-Cunningham doesn't come here very much, and he's not here now. He owns most of the shearing stations within a hundred mile radius, so he's probably at one of the others. But it doesn't make much difference because his wife pretty much runs this place.' So, Lucy, it turns out that I'm working for Fiona's parents, and it certainly seems like someone is trying to disrupt my life, just like they tried with Charlie."

"Oh, Bob." sighed Lucy. "I don't like to think people can be that way, but it's beginning to look like it. Just do the best you can. I have an idea that Mr. Forbes-Cunningham doesn't even know what's going on at the station, and maybe, when he *is* around, you can have a quiet talk with him."

"Yes, I'll keep a watch out for him, and try to work a little bit faster, too." replied Bob.

The next morning at the rink we got back into some serious training, because next on the agenda was the biggest event so far. The State Championships, this year in Bendigo. This is the qualifier for the National Championships, so both girls needed to do their very best because we knew that we were going to come up against better skaters that we'd encountered before. Apparently, this event has always been a very exciting competition with a large number of competitors, so I was looking forward to it immensely. Ralph Johnson said he had a brother living there, so he would come with us and do double-duty. Visiting some family members, and watching the skating competition. We were all very pleased that he was showing this much interest.

Right from the very first practice I could tell, from her demeanor, that Fiona was under tremendous pressure from her mother. Every time they were together she looked scared. Scared of the upcoming event, and her mother. This is not the best way to go about competing, but there was little I could do about it except remind Helen to be encouraging.

Skaters put themselves under tremendous pressure to perform well, so it really helps if the parents can give their children as much encouragement as possible at a competition.

I know as well as anyone that there is quite a lot at stake at competitions, but it bothers me when it's quite clear that the skater is getting no pleasure or enjoyment from competing. Many skaters I see nowadays look downright miserable. When I was in the British, European, and World championships I looked forward to competing, and enjoyed the company of my fellow competitors. Of course we all wanted to win, but it wasn't life or death, which is becoming more and more the case these days.

The practice session went well, but I could see we had some serious rivals. These other girls meant business and were skating their hearts out.

That evening, Ralph invited all the Warragong Springs skaters and parents out to dinner, but Helen graciously declined.

"Thank you, Ralph, but Fiona and I are going to have a quiet dinner in our hotel room, away from all the excitement."

I could tell from the expression on Fiona's face that she would have much preferred to have been with us, but she had no say in the matter. To say she looked glum would have been an understatement. I was beginning to feel quite sorry for this girl.

Ralph and his brother picked a great restaurant. It was lively and cheerful, and we all sat down at one huge table.

"There's just about everything on this menu." said our smiling host, "So order anything you like. It's all being paid for by our fantastic skating classes, and we all know who we have to thank for that."

I smiled, and felt a little embarrassed.

Looking through the huge menu, I suddenly felt quite emotional when I saw one particular item...'Bangers & Mash'.

"What's the matter, Charlie?" said a surprised Lucy as she put her arm around my shoulders.

"It's...this." I replied, pointing to the item. "It just suddenly reminded me of the Bangers and Mash my mother loves making for me."

"Oh, well maybe you shouldn't order them if they'll make you feel sad."

"No." I said. "I think I will, because it will make me feel like I'm back in England while I'm eating them. I think I'm just a little homesick."

"There you go. And I'm going to order the same thing." replied Lucy.

The food came, and we all had a very pleasant time together. Naturally, the Bangers & Mash weren't like my mother makes, but they were darned close!

"You know, Mr. Johnson," I said. "I must say that I'm very impressed with the way skating is run in this country. Everything is very organized."

"Really, Charlie?" he replied. "I would have thought the British association would be the best, and most efficient."

"Well, things are getting much more 'state of the art' now, but it wasn't always like that. As a matter of fact, my coach told me about some of the earlier days of the NSA - the National Skating Association - in the nineteen sixties and seventies. In those days, the NSA had a very small office in Charterhouse School in London, which was founded a few hundred years ago. In fact, the office was just one room, and, as far as she could remember, just one very dedicated person running it. He was the secretary of the association, and anyone visiting would be confronted with piles of papers and documents on his desk and the floor, but he welcomed visitors and took great pride showing them a four-hundred year old mulberry bush in the courtyard, from which they were allowed to pick one berry."

"Well, I never." exclaimed Ralph Johnson. "But then you British certainly have the edge on us when it comes to history. Your Tower of London, I believe, is about a thousand years old?"

"Yes, that's right, Mr. Johnson. Maybe the very first English skating association had an office in there!"

We finished off a memorable dinner with some very nice coffee, and then returned to the hotel.

After a good night's sleep we all woke up ready to meet the day. At the rink there was a twenty minute warm up session about two hours before the actual competition. It's always nice when you can skate two or three hours before your event to stretch your legs, get the feel of the ice, and give your lungs a blow out.

Then it was time to get ready for the event. Nearly all the mothers had a case with them full of make-up, hair spray, hair dryers, and a host of other beauty items. You would think we were at a Hollywood movie studio. I watched, as they applied the base make-up, blush, did the eye brows and lashes, lipstick and lip gloss, hair spray and some fancy items in the hair. And probably more things I didn't even notice. All I can say is, I'm glad I'm a guy.

I think, in all countries, there are certain areas where the skating community is more knowledgeable, and enthusiastic, than in other areas, and Bendigo certainly fits the bill. The Bendigo skating fans filled the building, and you could feel the excitement in the air. When their local skaters came out onto the ice they absolutely raised the roof. This was going to be an exciting one, and I hoped that my skaters were not going to be overawed by the occasion.

To their credit, the local skaters were friendly with the skaters from out of town, and very helpful. It made for a pleasantly competitive atmosphere, and it felt good to be there. Even the temperature in the rink was pleasant, which always makes an event much more enjoyable for the audience.

There were sixteen skaters in this event and, once again, it was good that my two skaters were not in the same warm-up group. Fiona was in the second warm-up, and Jenny in the fourth, so I could give each one my undivided attention.

I was pleased to see that both girls looked confident and relaxed, for there is no way a skater can hope to be successful if they lack confidence. You have to *know* that everything is going to work, and that you have no doubts lurking in the back of your mind. My coach used to say to me that she would never ask me to do anything that she didn't think I could do really well. That gave me tremendous confidence, and I pass along the same advice to my skaters.

As frail as Fiona looked, she was, it turned out, quite a tough individual. She had her battle face on for this one, and wasn't going to take any prisoners.

"Fiona," I called out. "You look like you're ready to skate a big one, today."

"Oh, yes, Mr. Williams, I want this one badly."

"Good for you, Fiona." I replied. "You're made of the right stuff."

When Fiona's warm up group took to the ice, she burst into life and stroked around the rink like a girl possessed. Usually, I like the skater to come over to me after they've warmed up a couple of jumps, but Fiona was so full of energy I let her carry on warming up all her elements for the rest of the warm-up. When she came off the ice I handed her a bottle of water and she eagerly drank a few mouthfuls.

"Whoa, Fiona!" I cautioned. "Don't drink too much. You don't want a lot of water slopping around in your stomach when you skate."

"Oh, okay Mr. Williams. I did need that, though."

"That's okay. You'll be fine." I said.

Fiona had time to relax for a while until it was her time to skate. And skate she did! Every jump was executed brilliantly, and her spins were a delight to watch. She was, deservedly, proud of her performance.

"I hope my mother will be pleased with that." she said, looking rather worried.

"Well she certainly should be." I replied. "You couldn't have done any better."

Just then, her mother came down the stairs and gave Fiona a big hug. The look on Fiona's face was that of a little child who so badly needed some praise, and finally got it. She was loving every moment of being held in her mother's arms.

"I think she deserves a big ice cream, Helen." I said, with a big smile on my face.

"Oh, can I, mummy?" said Fiona anxiously.

"You certainly can, my darling. Get your skates off, and we'll go and get one." replied Helen.

I had never seen Fiona looking so happy. And it made me feel good, too.

I now had to get Jenny in the right frame of mind for her performance, so I had her walk out her program, making sure that she remembered every arm and body movement.

"Remember, Jenny, if you lose speed in your three-jump combination, settle for two. The last one's an edge jump, and you can't do that from a standstill."

"Okay, Mr. Williams. I'll watch out for it."

Jenny, too, looked great on the warm-up, and I had high hopes of her skating a clean program. There were two skaters before her, and then it was her turn.

"Okay, Jenny. Let's keep up the good work." I said, as she stepped onto the ice to skate.

Well, not only did she keep up the good work, she excelled herself, skating with a new finesse that made her look like an international skater. I had two great girls, and I saw two great performances. I couldn't have wished for more. My cup runneth over, indeed.

After Jenny had seen her marks, and acknowledged the applause of the audience, she took off her skates and then said,

"I want to watch the remaining skaters, Mr. Williams. A lot of them are good friends of mine."

"Okay, Jenny. I'll watch them with you." I replied.

As each girl landed a jump, or came out of a spin, Jenny cheered and clapped. She really did want everyone to skate well, which said a lot about her character.

Finally, the event was over and it was time for the award ceremony. The podium was taken out to center ice and a red carpet was laid down from the podium to where the skaters get on the ice. The crowd was still buzzing from watching the last group of skaters, but eventually they calmed down and the announcer spoke.

"Ladies and gentlemen, I'll now announce the three medalists in reverse order. In third place, representing the Bendigo Skating Club, Sharon Carstairs!"

There was a warm round of applause as she skated out and took a bow. Then, she waved at the audience to show her appreciation before stepping onto the podium.

"In second place, representing the Skating Club of Warragong Springs, Fiona Forbes-Cunningham!"

Fiona skated out onto the ice looking very dejected, but managed to pull herself together to take a bow.

"And now, in first place, the new State champion of Victoria, Jenny Atkins!"

There was a huge round of applause as she skated out to the podium. She turned and curtseyed gracefully, and then waved enthusiastically at the audience with both hands. When she got up on the podium Sharon Carstairs turned to her and shook her hand warmly. Fiona, however, didn't move a muscle and just stood there, deadpan, basically refusing to shake Jenny's hand.

It's understandable that Fiona was disappointed that she didn't win, but not shaking hands, or even acknowledging Jenny, was pure bad sportsmanship, and I was very disappointed in her. These are the times when a competitor has to swallow their pride, and do the right thing.

Historically, probably the most extreme example of bad sportsmanship was witnessed at the nineteen thirty-six Summer Olympic Games in Berlin, Germany. Jesse Owens won four gold medals, but Adolf Hitler, the German Chancellor, refused to shake hands and congratulate him at the medal ceremony because he was black. But enough of that.

After the medal ceremony was over, Helen was back to her old self and said, in her usual business-like manner,

"Well, Charles, I want you to work extra hard on Fiona in the time we have left before the National Championships. I wouldn't like to think that you favored Jenny over Fiona, but it's rather looking that way."

I could have answered, and tried to make her see sense, but there was really no point. There is an old saying that goes, "A man convinced against his will, is of the same opinion still." Well, this happened to be a woman, but it still applied.

Helen then went and mingled with some of the other parents, and I didn't have to be a lip-reader to see that she was making disparaging remarks to all who would listen. I hoped they weren't about me. She had become more and more upset ever since Fiona started finishing second to Jenny, and could no longer contain herself.

If the spoken word is powerful enough to start and finish wars, you can imagine the damage it can do to a coach's reputation.

After the girls had changed and come out of the dressing room, Helen pulled Fiona to one side and said,

"Don't worry, Fiona. You know, all sorts of things can happen in life, so let's see what the future holds. Jenny may be winning the battles, but we're going to win the war."

Well, that was another competition under our belt, and I was very pleased to see my two girls finish first and second again, despite the strong opposition. Jenny had won, and Fiona was second, but this time the gap between them was wider. I wasn't looking forward to seeing Helen's reaction to that, but as it turned out, I didn't have to. The top three skaters were supposed to attend an informal meeting with the news reporters, but Helen made Fiona pack her things quickly, and then whisked her out of the rink without even staying for it. I had to make up an excuse when the officials asked me why she wasn't present to meet the press.

"I'm so sorry about that." I said, apologetically. "I think there's an illness in the family." And I don't think I was far wrong.

As the state of Victoria had most of the good skaters at this time, and I'd now seen the best of them, my hopes were high that one of my girls might win the national title.

The drive home was a long one, about two hundred and fifty miles, but it's always so much more bearable when you're a winner. It's a comfortable four hour drive, and I must say I felt quite at home because in Australia they drive on the left, the same as in England.

As far as I know, most of Australia is very flat, dry, and open, so it was refreshing to see Lake Tyrrell about halfway home from Bendigo, even though it was almost dry at this time of year. It's a huge lake covering about fifty-one thousand acres, and my traveling companions told me that it's usually covered in about two inches of water in winter. When the water evaporates it leaves a crust of salt which is harvested by a company in Sea Lake, a town about four miles from the lake. Now, I know as much about Lake Tyrrell as anyone else!

Upon my return from Bendigo I was pleased to see a letter waiting for me.

Dear Charlie,

How are you? I'm guessing you're feeling well, and doing well by the sound of things. Your dad and I are pleased that you've found a nice place to work, but, obviously, we miss you a lot. Thanks for your last letter. It's nice that you keep us up to date on what's happening over there, because, naturally, we worry about you.

We have no idea what it's like in Warragong Springs but it sounds like a very friendly place, and a lot less hectic than London. Your dad says you can always tell when you're in a small town because when you plug in your electric razor, the street lights dim.

We haven't heard any more about Jimmy since his father was sent to prison, and nobody from the association has contacted us. It's as though you don't even exist in their minds any more, but they're going to feel very embarrassed when the truth comes out. Everyone you know here has either called us, or visited us, and told us that they're solidly behind you, so that should make you feel better.

If you're going to be there for a fairly long time, maybe dad and I can come out and see you one day, but that wouldn't be for a while I'm afraid, so do you think you might be able to fly back after the Australian Championships for a week or two? That would be so nice, but we don't want to spoil anything for you over there.

Take care of yourself, and keep up the good work.

All our love,
Mum and dad.

This was just what I needed. Because, right now, there was so much going on in my life, and it's all too easy to get caught up in the excitement of everything that's going on. There's my students, the new friends I've made, and the new things I'm doing. And then I get a letter from good ol' mum and dad, and it reminds me about one of the most important values in life. Family. I may be thousands of miles away from them, but they're my family, always there for me, providing that solid security. A safety net, if you will. And always totally unselfish. God bless 'em!

The next few days went by very pleasantly. I acquired even more new students and got into a nice rhythm of teaching. This meant I was earning a decent living, so my trips to the Warragong Springs Bank and Trust were becoming more frequent.

"Good morning, Meg." I said to one of the tellers.

"G'day Charlie." she replied. "How's it going at the rink?"

"Oh, really good, thanks. And how's your brother's knee? Has it healed up yet?"

Her brother, Tom, had been in a dirt bike accident a few days before, and she had told me all about it.

"Yes, it's almost healed, but it's going to leave him with a bit of a scar. Then again, he's got scars all over his body, so it won't even notice."

"Well, I suppose that's going to happen when you race a dirt bike. I'll stick to ice skating. It's definitely a lot safer!"

Just then, the manager came out of his office.

"Hello, Charlie. How's my boy doing in his skating lessons?"

"Oh, he's doing great, Robert. He just learned how to do a loop jump yesterday. He's a fast learner."

"I'm glad to hear that. Keep up the good work."

Things were definitely not as informal as this when I used to visit my London bank. There, it was Mr. Williams, Miss Clark, Miss Harrison, and so on. And almost no-one smiled.

15

A CONTEST OF A DIFFERENT NATURE

~⁓⁓⁓⁓⁓~

Before I knew it, it was Saturday morning, and I was enjoying a nice sleep in. But all good things must come to an end.

"Charlie? Are you awake yet?"

"Oh, no. Is that you, Billy?"

"Well who do you think it is? Your fairy godmother? Come on, get out of bed. We're going to cheer on Jenny's dad at the sheep-shearing contest."

"Oh...yes." I replied, opening one eye. "Alright, let me get a shave and a shower and I'll be ready soon."

"Okay. Mum said breakfast will be ready in twenty minutes."

As usual, a hot shower did the trick, and by the time I went down to breakfast I felt on top of the world.

"You're looking pretty perky this morning." remarked Billy's mum.

"Yes. I think it must be due to this new life I'm living. I feel so happy and relaxed, now."

"Well here's a nice big English breakfast for you." she replied, putting it down in front of me.

"Mmm, yummy!"

I had to admit to myself, these Australian mums can certainly serve up some good food.

After breakfast it was time to hit the road for the sheep-shearing station. We all piled into, and onto, the pick-up truck. I say onto, because there were several more people going with us, and as there wasn't room for everyone inside, the remaining ones sat on the rear platform holding onto a very large crate of beer. For stability, of course. If nothing else, it stopped them falling off the side of the truck.

As we approached the station we could see flags flying, and bunting everywhere. It seemed like hundreds of people were converging on the place, and you could already feel the excitement in the air. This was a big occasion in Warragong Springs, and the townsfolk were not going to miss it for anything. Parking was organized to begin with, but then it got completely out of hand, and people just left their vehicles wherever they wanted. It was that sort of occasion.

Bob was already there, oiling his shearing equipment in readiness for the first round of the contest.

"Hi Bob!" I called out. "Are you all ready for the event?"

"Yes, Charlie. But now listen. You're a sports coach, so what last minute advice do you have for me?".

"You're not serious, are you, Bob?" I replied.

"Of course I am. Now what would you tell Jenny?"

"Well, I'd tell her to maintain really good posture, and smile at the judges to look confident. But we both know that's not going to help you one little bit."

"Yeah, of course, Charlie. I was just joking with you. If I don't know what I've got to do today, I might as well give up."

"You'll be great, Bob." I reassured him. "You've got a whole lot of supporters here and I'm really glad I could come. I've never seen anything like this, so it's going to be very interesting. And, like most things, I'm sure there's a technique involved."

Bob smiled and nodded.

"Oh, yes. We don't just shear them any old how. The way you hold the sheep is important. And let me tell you, Charlie, Jenny's not the only one who needs to have good footwork. It's very important in our job, too. We hold the sheep between our legs, and have our toes turned in or out, depending on how we want to position the sheep. Then we need to shear it's flat surfaces, so we have to position the sheep so that we can do that. We start at the belly, and then work our way around. There's a pattern. And when they've been shorn, they should look as smooth as a shelled hard-boiled egg. No ridges, no cuts. We have to go for speed, but not at the expense of quality."

I was quite taken aback by this information.

"Well, this is an eye-opener for me."

"And then," Bob continued, "Would you believe that there have been politics involved, union unrest, and even violence in the shearing industry?"

"Really? Go on, Bob. I'm dying to hear about this."

"Well, back around nineteen eighty-three we had the 'Wide Comb Dispute'."

"What on earth was that?" I asked.

"It was when some bloke started using a wider comb and cutter for shearing. It was only just over an inch wider than the one everyone else was using, but the unions said that it wasn't fair to the rest of the workers because it gave an unfair advantage, enabling the shearer to shear more sheep per hour. People became very divided over this matter, and fights broke out between both sides, resulting in quite a few bloodied noses. Eventually, they worked out a solution, but it was tense for a while."

"Well," I replied. "I learn something new every day."

Lucy took me over to the notice board to see the list of competitors. She ran her finger down the list until she came to Bob.

"There he is. Number fifty-three. So it'll be about a hour before he competes. Why don't you let me show you around the station? You've probably never seen one before."

"No, I haven't. Let's go."

Lucy gave me quite the professional tour before we went back to get a good seat for the competition.

Jenny was already seated with a group of her school friends. And they were a noisy bunch!

"Hi, Mr. Williams!" they yelled out in chorus.

"Hi, girls." I replied. "Save your voices for Jenny's dad. We've got to make sure he knows he's got some supporters."

"We will."

It wasn't long before we heard Bob's name announced.

"Ladies and gentlemen, our next contestant, number fifty-three, Bob Atkins."

A great cheer went up from our group as Bob waved to the crowd. Then, they opened the door of the pen and Bob dragged the sheep out and started shearing.

Lucy jumped up to her feet and started yelling,

"Go on, Bob! Go on, Bob!"

I'd never seen Lucy so excited. She was going nuts!

Bob seemed to be shearing very efficiently, and it wasn't long before he'd finished his first sheep. So far, so good. Each contestant had to shear three sheep, working against the clock, and the three times would then be added up. The shearer with the lowest total time would be the winner.

Bob had about thirty minutes between shearing each sheep, so he had time to come over and sit with us.

"Wow, Bob. You made it look so easy." I said.

"Well that was a fairly quiet one. Some of them wriggle like crazy."

Here, Bob," said Lucy. "There's some nice hot tea in this Thermos."

Bob took it and enjoyed a well-earned drink.

"Thanks, Lucy. That'll set me up nicely for the next sheep."

About twenty minutes later, a voice called out from the shed.

"Bob. 'you almost ready?"

"Yes, Jack. I'll be right there. Gotta go, folks. Wish me luck."

Bob went back and waited for his cue.

A couple of minutes later the man gave Bob a signal and opened the pen. Bob grabbed the sheep and dragged it out to the shearing machine. This sheep had a bit more spirit, but Bob wedged it between his legs and got on with the shearing. His final time was only one second slower than with the first sheep, so he was still looking good for a medal, so to speak.

After another cup of tea Bob went back and sheared his final sheep, and this one was done in a faster time than the other two.

"Oh my goodness," Lucy exclaimed, shaking from head to foot. "He may have done really well in this competition."

"I know how you feel, Lucy," I said. "But try to calm down. This is exactly how we skating coaches feel when our skater has come off the ice, and we have to wait for the result. It can be agonizing."

It did take quite a while for them to calculate the result but eventually Michael Corcoran, the man hosting the event, picked up the microphone.

"Ladies and gentlemen, I will now announce the result of this year's Machine Shearing contest, and I'll name the top three in reverse order. In third place, and I'm proud to say, one of the longest standing shearers at this station...Ed Sheehan!"

A great cheer went up for one of the best liked men in the area.

"And, in second place, another pretty good bloke...John McNair!"

Another great cheer, this time from a different section of the audience.

"And a deserved first place goes to a relatively new kid on the block, but a welcome one...Bob Atkins!"

A huge cheer went up, with no-one cheering louder than Lucy, but a few seconds later she feinted. She keeled right over and fell off her chair.

"Mum!" yelled Jenny. "Are you alright?"

Lucy, obviously, didn't hear Jenny, but after a couple of minutes she started to come 'round, feeling very embarrassed.

Meanwhile, Bob was receiving a little trophy they made for the occasion.

"Congratulations, Bob!" said the host. "We want to present you with this trophy, and hope that you'll find a nice place to display it in your home. That was a fantastic display of shearing, and we're mighty glad to have you here on the station. Would you like to say a few words to these wonderful people?"

"I certainly would, Michael," said Bob, taking the microphone. "First of all, thank you so much for this lovely trophy. I'll treasure it for the rest of my life, and it's going to go right in the middle of the mantlepiece in our living room. And, secondly, I want to thank the owner of this station for holding this contest, and all the great people of Warragong Springs who came out to support this event. You're a great bunch of people, and I'm very happy to be living here, now."

There was a nice round of applause as Bob shook hands with the host and then came over to where we were sitting.

"Your dad's more famous than you, now, Jenny." I said, smiling.

"Oh, I'm fine with that, Mr. Williams. I want him to be the most famous shearer in Australia."

Bob then went to see if Lucy was alright.

"Are you okay, Lucy?"

"Yes, Bob. I'm fine, now. I guess I just got a little too overexcited."

"Well I don't know. It's been a long time since a women feinted at the sight of *me*."

"Well, you *are* my handsome husband." replied Lucy, giving him a big kiss on the cheek.

Bob's face went beet red as Jenny and her friends let out a chorus.

"Aaaahhh..."

Shortly after that, the foreman came over and shook Bob's hand.

"Well done, Bob. I must say, that was quite an impressive display of shearing."

"Well, thank you, boss. This *is* a surprise."

"Yes, well, er...you have to understand that I've been under a lot of pressure here to push all of you to the maximum."

He turned to walk away, but then turned around and said,

"You're doing alright, Bob."

"Thanks, boss."

Bob knew that he was the only one who had been pressured, but he also realized what the foreman was trying to say.

It had already been a great morning, but Bob had one more pleasant surprise in store. The competition host came running over just as we were preparing to leave.

"Oh, I'm glad I caught you before you left, Bob. At the trophy ceremony we completely forgot to hand out the envelopes with the prize money. Here you are." he said, handing Bob his envelope.

"Well, I wasn't expecting this, but thank you. Thank you very much." replied Bob.

"Enjoy the rest of your day, and I hope we'll see you here again next year. Good on yer, mate."

"Oh, yes," Bob assured him. "I'll definitely be back."

When we got back in the truck, Bob opened the envelope.

"Blimey, Lucy, there's enough here for me to get new tires for this truck, and more. What a turn-up."

Lucy put her arms around Bob and hugged him.

"Oh, Bob. It seems like everything's starting to work out right for us. And it looks like there'll be some money left over to help us hold a party after Nationals for Jenny, whether she finishes first or last."

On the road back to Warragong Springs, it didn't take long to realize that there was an obvious reason for that crate of beer being in the truck. And very welcome it was, too!

16

DESPERATE MEASURES

The last few days had been very exciting, but now I had to put the finishing touches on what had been a very successful season so far. An important part of my job as a championship coach was to know exactly how much training my skaters needed, so the onus was now on me. We had some time before Nationals to get in some good training, but if I drove them too hard by making them run through their programs too many times each week, or if I kept them on the ice for long hours, they could become jaded and stale. I had to come up with a perfect plan whereby they would work hard enough, but still be fresh when they competed at the championships. A nice balance of training enough, but not too much, because they're human beings and not machines.

I decided to cut down on their strength training at the gym and increase their cardio-vascular workouts. They already had good muscle tone but could afford to be even fitter than they were. I increased their stretching exercises and had them walk out their programs in front of a mirror to work on their expression and body movement.

The weeks went by, and suddenly it was time for all the hard work to bear fruit.

The plan was to drive to Melbourne the next morning, skate an afternoon practice, get some rest, and be ready to practice and compete the following day. But things don't always go according to plan.

At the usual time, Jenny came out of her school near the sheep shearing station, and started walking the two miles to the rink for a final practice.

After she'd walked half a mile, a pickup truck drew alongside and the driver called out,

"Hello Jenny, it's much too hot today. Jump in and we'll drop you off at the rink. You know me, don't you? I'm Chris, and I work at the garage in town."

"Oh, yes. Thanks. I'll take you up on the lift."

Jenny sat in the passenger seat, but didn't notice another man in the back seat behind her. He spoke.

"I'm John. Chris's brother."

"Oh my God!" said Jenny, startled. "I didn't know anyone was in the back seat."

"That's alright. Just relax, and we'll be at the rink soon."

As they drove off, Jenny laid her head back and closed her eyes. When Chris saw this, he turned to John and nodded his head. John then took a plastic bag out of his pocket and opened it. Inside it was a wad of cloth. He took it out and slowly leaned forward towards Jenny. Checking that her eyes were still closed, he stealthily brought the wad of cloth around in front of Jenny's face and then, quick as lightning, pulled it back tightly over her nose and mouth.

"MMMPH! MMMPH!" Jenny gasped, as her eyes flashed open, horrified. She tried to pull his hand away from her face but by now Chris had stopped the truck and was holding both of her arms so that she couldn't get free. She started kicking out and put up a fierce struggle, but the drug-soaked cloth was starting to have an effect. Slowly, her muffled cries died down to a whimper, and she became limp, slumping forward onto the dashboard.

"Alright. Good work, John." said Chris, getting back in the driver's seat. He put the truck into gear and roared away at high speed. About half a mile down the road he turned onto a dirt road that led up to an old farmhouse where he stopped and parked.

"Okay. We gotta be quick." said Chris. "That drug will only keep her unconscious for about thirty minutes, so we gotta get her tied up before it wears off."

The two men carried her lifeless body into an old shed at the back of the house, and then laid her down on a camp bed. They taped her ankles together, tied her hands behind her back, and tied an extra cord between her ankles and wrists so that she couldn't stand up unless they untied it.

"That one's to make sure she doesn't go hopping out of here like a bloomin' kangaroo." said Chris. Then he went outside.

"Alice!" he shouted, in the direction of the farmhouse. A hefty-looking woman came out and walked toward the shed.

"We've got her! Now, make sure the food and water's ready, and when she comes 'round show her where the toilet is."

Chris took a Polaroid camera out of a drawer and proceeded to take several photographs of Jenny from different angles.

"Right, that should be good enough proof that we got her. Our client should be more than pleased with these photos. Now, look after her, Alice. We've got to keep her alive. Kidnapping's bad enough, but we don't want to be on a murder charge."

He then made sure each photograph was dry before putting them into a envelope.

"Okay, my dear sister," said Chris, smiling, "We're going into town to collect the money we've been promised."

Chris and John went out to their truck and drove off to complete their business deal. Meanwhile, back in the shed, Jenny was starting to regain consciousness.

"Ooh...ooh. Where am I?"

"That'd be telling, wouldn't it, you little brat." said Alice.

Jenny's eyes opened slowly, and she looked around. Then she focused on Alice.

"Who are you? What am I doing here?"

"We thought you needed a little change of scenery, so shut up and stop asking questions!"

"Why am I tied up? What's going on? I'm skating in the National Championships the day after tomorrow."

"Is that so? Well, unless they're going to hold the championships in this shed, I'd say you've got a bit of a problem."

Jenny stared across the room and began to realize what was happening.

"You can't keep me here. This isn't fair." said Jenny, angrily.

Alice moved closer to her and looked her square in the eye.

"Life isn't fair, sweetie, so listen! When you're hungry, I'll give you food. When you're thirsty, I'll give you water. And when you need to go to the toilet, I'll undo the cord behind you and take you there. These are the rules for the next forty-eight hours, so shut up and get used to them!"

She sat Jenny up on the camp bed and made her drink some water.

"You won't be too uncomfortable, and you've even got a T.V. to watch. Are you hungry, yet?"

"No. I don't want anything."

"You'll change your mind by this time tomorrow, my girl."

Jenny just rolled her eyes and then slumped down sideways on the camp bed. When she saw that Alice wasn't watching she tried to free her hands. She pulled and pulled, but it was no use. The twine was tight around her wrists and she just ended up chafing her skin until it bled. She gave up, and fell asleep for a couple of hours. When she woke up, Alice was still sitting there, so Jenny swallowed her pride and spoke up.

"I am hungry now. Can I have something to eat?"

"Yeah, okay. I'll go and make you a sandwich and a cup of tea, but don't try anything."

Alice got up and went into the house. When Jenny was sure that she couldn't be seen, she sat up and looked around the shed for something - anything - that she could use to cut the twine that bound her wrists. On the shelves there were pots of paint, brushes, a hammer and nails, but no knives or blades. Then, in the far corner on the floor, she saw an old rusty wood saw, the sort they use to cut down trees. She figured out that it would take her about five or ten minutes to crawl and wriggle her way across the floor, but there was no telling how long it would take to hold the saw in place behind her back and rub the twine on the blade to cut herself free. She would have to choose the perfect moment to perform this task, but when would this be, if ever?

Jenny had to set her thoughts aside as Alice returned with a tray of food. She put it on a small table by the camp bed and asked,

"What do you want? Ham or cheese?"

"Ham...please."

Alice picked up a ham sandwich and held it in front of Jenny's mouth. Jenny leaned forward and took a bite.

"Is it good?" Alice asked.

Jenny, with her mouth full, merely nodded.

"I can make more if you're still hungry after this one, because I've got nothing to do except watch over you like a bloomin' nursemaid. Our main object is to keep you alive until we release you, and then we're outta here."

Over the next few minutes Jenny finished the sandwich, and then Alice held the mug of tea up to Jenny's mouth so that she could drink from it.

"You want another sandwich?" asked Alice.

"No thanks. That was plenty for now." replied Jenny.

Alice sat silently for a while, and then turned on the television.

"May as well see what's going on in the world, not that it matters." she said, cynically.

A few minutes later the Six 'o' clock news came on. The announcer started reading the news and then suddenly hesitated.

"We have some breaking news, and it's quite disturbing. Jenny Atkins, the girl who's favorite to win the National Ice Skating title in Melbourne this weekend, has disappeared. She failed to turn up for practice today at the Warragong Springs ice rink, and a huge search is now going on in the area. And now, we've just heard that the rink received an anonymous phone call a few minutes ago, saying that she is alive and well, but that they wouldn't say any more than that. Police are now suspecting that she might have been kidnapped."

Jenny's mouth dropped open, and tears started to run down her cheeks.

She turned to Alice and glared daggers at her.

"Why have you done this? Why do you hate me? What have I ever done to you?"

Alice, in a much more mellow tone than before, answered,

"I don't hate you, Jenny. I don't hate you at all. But all our lives my two brothers and I have never had a penny to spare, and then we were told we could make some easy money, and a lot of it, in a very short time. Enough for the three of us to get out of this country and start a whole new life. So that's the story."

"Well, I hope you're proud of yourself." replied Jenny, sobbing.

An hour or so later, Jenny had another sandwich and some more tea, but realized that her body was now starting to cramp and stiffen. It wasn't used to being confined like this. It was used to moving freely, and stretching and rotating, and feeling active, but now almost every muscle in her body was aching, and she was beginning to despair of ever being rescued. She tried laying in different positions to move whatever parts of her body she could, and tried deep breathing to help her blood circulation, but it wasn't much help. She was completely helpless, and it was a horrible feeling.

"Please, please untie me." she pleaded again and again, but the response was always the same.

"No can do, Jenny. It'd be more than my life's worth."

Just when Jenny had all but given up hope, the phone rang in the house. Jenny's mind started racing. She tried to think about a possible way of escaping if Alice went out to the house.

"I wonder who the hell that can be?" said Alice, getting up to go into the house. She left the shed door open behind her, and the house door open when she went in. Jenny could just about hear Alice answering.

"Hello. Who is it? Bruce? Oh, for Christ's sake, Bruce, you picked a bloody awful time to call me. I've got some serious business going on here right now."

There was a pause while she listened to what Bruce had to say, but from then on, Alice got into a lengthy argument which, Jenny figured, might take up some valuable time. Jenny's heart started pounding when she realized it was now or never, and knew it was a race against time. She thought to herself,

"Keep arguing, lady. You look just the type that would argue the hind leg off a donkey."

She rolled off the camp bed onto the floor and started wriggling and twisting to slowly edge towards the other side of the shed. Even though it was exhausting, she felt that she could make it, but halfway across the floor she heard Alice yell into the phone.

"Well, you'd better send that alimony check this week or I'll have you in court next week." Then she heard Alice slam down the phone.

"Oh, no!" thought Jenny. "She's coming back. I've got to get back to the bed before she comes in."

She wriggled as hard as she could, and got herself up on the bed just as Alice walked in.

"Why are *you* looking so tired out?" said Alice.

Jenny thought quickly, and then said,

"Oh...I was just moving my body about as much as I could to keep the circulation going."

"Don't bother. You'll live." came the sarcastic reply.

About an hour later Chris and John came back, carrying a crate of beer.

"We're back," Chris said to Alice. "So you can get three or four hours sleep while we watch her."

"Okay, but first I'll take her to the toilet so she'll be okay for a few hours." said Alice. "We're not going to untie your ankles, Jenny, so you're going to have to hop, but I'll hold your arm so you don't fall over."

"That's right." said Chris. "Kangaroos do it, so why shouldn't she?"

Alice untied the cord behind Jenny's back and helped her to stand up. Then she held Jenny's arm as she hopped over to the door and outside to the toilet.

When they came back inside the shed, Alice said,

"I'm going into the house now to get some sleep, so I'll set my alarm for ten p.m. and see you in about three hours."

"Okay, Alice. See you then." replied Chris.

The two brothers settled down and opened some bottles of beer.

"You want a beer, Jenny?" asked John, laughing.

"No, I don't. I don't drink beer. I'm only fourteen."

"You don't know what you're missing. I know lots of fourteen year old girls, and they all drink beer."

Jenny sensed there was something strange about John, and thought that, maybe, he had a mental problem.

"Leave her alone, John, and drink your beer." said Chris.

An hour went by, and the two brothers opened more bottles.

John, who had already drunk three bottles of beer, stared at Jenny for a long time. Then a smile came across his face.

"You know, Chris, the more beer I drink, the prettier Jenny looks."

When Jenny heard this, she froze, and felt very scared.

"No, John...No! Don't be a fool." said Chris, sternly. "We're returning her in exactly the same condition as when we kidnapped her."

"Alright, alright...spoilsport." replied John. "Let's have another beer."

For the next hour or so Jenny glanced at them occasionally, noticing that they were getting more and more drunk. She watched as John's eyes slowly closed. Then, his head dropped back and he slumped over sideways on the sofa, his mouth hanging wide open. The bottle he was holding slipped through his fingers and fell onto the floor. Luckily, not loud enough to wake him.

Jenny said a quiet prayer to herself that Chris, too, would fall asleep soon, and about five minutes later he did just that. It looked like they were both out cold, so Jenny said another prayer. This time, that she could escape.

17

Softly, Softly, Catchee Wood Saw

Ten p.m.! Alice's alarm clock was going to go off at ten p.m., but to Jenny it wasn't an alarm clock, it was a time bomb. She knew that as long as the brothers didn't wake up, she would have until then to get away from this nightmare, but what time was it now? Luckily, there was a clock on the table. She figured that Alice must have put it there to be able to see the time while she was watching her. It was now nine-fifteen, so Jenny had a bit less than forty-five minutes to get free.

Once again, she rolled off the bed onto the floor, this time as quietly as she could, and then started to wriggle her way over to the other side of the shed, glancing back at the brothers to make sure they were still asleep.

Inch by inch, and foot by foot, she managed to get halfway across the floor in, what she considered, record time. She looked back at the clock. Nine twenty-two. Just about on schedule, she thought. But the floor was dirty, and her clothes became covered in dust, and the dust was starting to get up her nose. She realized she was going to sneeze. She put her head down near her shoulder and sneezed as quietly as she could, but did Chris or John hear her? She looked 'round. Thank God, they were still sleeping. Then she started wriggling again until she reached the saw.

"Now what do I do?" she thought. "I'm going to have to be a contortionist to get the saw positioned behind me and get my wrists on the blade."

She thought for a while and then managed to get up on her knees. A quick look at the clock showed it to be nine thirty. Then she turned her back to the saw and reached back with her hands to get hold of it. The next thing was to put one end of it between her calf muscles, and then grip it tightly to hold it steady. Mission accomplished! The blade was now vertical so she carefully reached back until her wrists were on each side of the blade, with the twine *on* the blade.

"Oh my God. What time is it now?" She took another quick look at the clock. Nine thirty-five! "Oh, God. I'm never going to make it."

Trying not to cut her wrists on the sharp serrations of the blade, she started rubbing the twine up and down. The worst thing was that she couldn't even see if the strands of twine were being cut. It didn't feel like they were.

"Oh, my God." she thought to herself. "This is much harder than I thought it would be, but I've got to keep trying. If I can just do it, I can be free."

Jenny was now sweating profusely, and her arms were aching as she used the last ounces of energy she had. Up and down she rubbed, harder and harder, and then, suddenly, her hopes were raised. Some of the strands of twine were breaking.

"Yes. I can do it! I must be close to getting it all."

She rested for about thirty seconds and then looked at the clock again. Nine forty-five!

Putting everything she had into it, she rubbed more frantically than ever, cutting her wrists a couple times. She could feel the trickles of blood running down her hands but she didn't care. She had to keep going. Victory was in sight. Her hard work was about to pay dividends because, all of a sudden, the remaining strands of twine broke and her hands became free. Then she realized it wasn't all good news.

"Oh, no. I can hardly move my arms. They've been pinned behind me for so long."

Her muscles were aching, and she had never felt so sore. Gradually, Jenny made some circular movements with her arms to get some feeling back in them. What time was it? Nine fifty-four! Then she undid the cord and cut the tape off her ankles with the saw. She was free! At least it seemed like it. She was relieved that her hands and ankles were free, but then she realized that *she* wasn't. She still had to find a way of getting away from there. If Alice heard her from the house, it was all over. She stood up, and found that every part of her body was stiff and aching. Then she took one last look at those evil brothers and crept quietly to the door. A last glance at the clock showed it to be nine fifty-eight. She carefully opened the door and went outside, walking as quietly as she could past the house and onto the dirt road. Even walking hurt, but she knew the alarm clock was going to ring any second now, so she figured that running couldn't be any worse.

Just as she started running down the dirt road she heard the alarm clock go off. She turned around and saw Alice moving about upstairs in the house. Jenny figured it would only be a few minutes before Alice came down and discovered her sleeping brothers, and then they would surely come after her. The bad news was, she was on foot, and they had a truck.

As it was dark, she had no idea how long the dirt road was, so she just kept running. After a couple of minutes she was exhausted, and stopped for a quick breather. At that moment, she wished she had been in training for track and field instead of ice skating.

Once she got her breath back she started off again, running at an even pace, glancing over her shoulder every few seconds. Then, up ahead, she could see the headlights of several cars, which meant that she must be getting near to a proper road.

She reached the road and flagged down the next car that came along.

"My God, what happened to you?" said the driver.

"I'll tell you as we go along, but please take me to the police station."

"Right. No worries. Jump in."

On the way to the police station Jenny told the man about her horrible experience, but she had no idea of knowing what was going on back at the shed.

Unbeknownst to Jenny, Alice was in no rush to relieve her brothers of their three hour shift, and didn't go out to the shed for nearly ten minutes. When she did, all hell broke loose.

"Chris! John! Wake up, you stupid idiots. She's gone! You've both fallen asleep, and she's got away!"

Chris opened his eyes. He was in a daze.

"Why didn't you keep an eye on her, John?" Chris said, accusingly.

"Well...Why didn't *you*? Why do I always get the blame?" replied John.

Chris slapped John's head.

"Because you're bloody stupid, that's why."

"Oh, God! My head feels bad enough without you doing that."

Alice looked across the floor.

"Well look at that. She managed to get over to the saw and cut herself loose, the clever little brat. And look at the blood on the floor. Might be better for us if she bleeds to death. Come on, let's get in the truck and see if we can catch up with her. She may not be too far away."

The three of them rushed out to the truck and took off down the dirt road. As they drove along, Chris said,

"What are we going to tell Mrs. Forbes-Cunningham? She's paid us, and we haven't delivered the goods. And she's not a woman you want to get on the wrong side of. She knows some dangerous people."

"Alright, alright." replied Alice, anxiously. "Let's see if we can find Jenny, first. We don't need to contact that lady until the last minute."

By now, Jenny had reached the police station.

"Thank you *so* much for bringing me here. You may well have saved my life. What's your name? I want to tell my mum and dad."

"Trevor Matthews. I work at the sheep-shearing station."

"So does my dad! Oh, well, he'll find you, then. Thanks again!"

"You're welcome, girl. Good on yer!"

Jenny went into the police station and immediately saw a familiar face.

"Sergeant Cooper. It's me, Jenny."

"Jenny! You're safe! What happened? You look like you've just gone ten rounds with the heavyweight champion."

"Well, can you first call my mum and dad? They must be worried sick about me."

Sergeant Cooper picked up the phone and called them. Then he put down the phone.

"Your mum and dad are on their way, and they are mightily relieved."

"I'll bet they are." replied Jenny, smiling.

Five minutes later Jenny's parents ran into the police station.

"Oh, my baby, my baby!" said a tearful Lucy, hugging Jenny like she never had before. "We thought we might never see you again. So you *were* kidnapped. What vicious people...whoever they are. Are you okay? Are you okay?"

Then it was Bob's turn to give his daughter a hug.

"Looks to me like you've been climbing trees again."

"No, dad." replied Jenny, bursting into tears.

"Don't worry, my sweet." said Bob, hugging her again. "We'll get to the bottom of all this, but first we want to make sure you're not injured or hurting in any way."

"No, I'll be okay." assured Jenny. "I've been tied up for a long time and I'm really sore all over, but that's all. And I know it sounds crazy, but I still want to skate in the championship, although I'll probably feel even worse when I wake up tomorrow morning."

At that point, Sergeant Cooper interrupted.

"Bob, I have to tell you that, in a kidnapping situation like this, I can't release Jenny until the Federal Police have interviewed her, and that may not be until tomorrow morning." Then he thought for a moment.

"Then again, as Jenny is underage, and because I know you, it *is* in my power to release her under your supervision. But, Jenny, just give me some brief details about what happened so that I can forward them to the Superintendent at the Federal Police. They're going to want to start tracking down the kidnappers as soon as possible. Then, he can meet with you on Monday and you can fill in the rest of the details."

Jenny related the most important details of the kidnapping and then added,

"When they arrest Alice, can they go a bit easy on her? She did feed me, and I'm sure she felt bad about me being kidnapped."

"Well, Jenny." replied Sergeant Cooper. "If she's apprehended, along with her two brothers, she'll have to face justice, but I'm sure those facts will be brought to light in the trial."

As soon as Bob and Lucy had got Jenny home, they contacted the championship officials to tell them that all was well, and that Jenny would be competing.

Lucy looked at her bedraggled daughter and said,

"Let's get these wounds cleaned up, and then you can take a good shower to get all that dirt off you. Then I'll get you something to eat."

"Okay. Thanks, mum. Anything but a ham sandwich."

18

THE DAY OF THE CHAMPIONSHIPS DAWNS

Helen and Fiona arrived at the arena about three hours before the Ladies event.

As they walked into the arena, Fiona remarked,

"You seem very happy, Mummy. You must think we're going to have a very good day."

"Oh, I *know* we're going to have a very good day!" replied Helen, smugly.

"Now, you go down to the dressing rooms and wait for Charlie. He'll be here soon to get you nicely warmed up. I'm going to have some lunch here on the main level."

Helen bought a sandwich and some coffee and sat down to enjoy it. It pleased her to see large crowds of people filing in from the street because, she thought to herself, they would be seeing her daughter become Australian champion.

She had almost finished her sandwich when a look of horror came over her face. Her mouth dropped open as she saw Jenny and her parents walking through the door. For a second, she froze. Then she jumped up and rushed over to a pay phone. Frantically, she dialed a number and waited for them to answer.

"You bloody fools! Why didn't you tell me? The girl must have escaped because she's here in the arena! I can't do anything, myself, so think of something! I'll stay by the phone."

Ten minutes later she received a call back.

"Mrs. Forbes-Cunningham? It's Chris. I'm sorry we messed up, but don't worry. I know two men in Melbourne who will do the job. They're not far from the arena and will be leaving very soon. These guys work fast, but they just need to know what she's wearing. They know the goods delivery entrance at the back of the arena, and they'll get in that way, dressed as delivery men. Then, it won't be too difficult for them to find the right moment to grab Jenny and take her away in their van. We can still get her."

"Well, this had better work. Call them and tell them that she's wearing a big yellow coat with 'Warragong Springs' written on the front and back of it. And tell them they'll be well paid."

"Okay, Mrs. Forbes-Cunningham. It'll be done."

Down in the dressing room area Jenny had started to try to loosen up her aching body with every exercise she could think of.

"Wow, these exercises are making me sweat."

"I wish *I* felt warmer." replied Fiona, sitting curled up on a bench. "I'm freezing."

Jenny could see that Fiona was shivering, so she took off her coat.

"Here, put this on. You'll be as warm as I am in a couple of minutes."

"Thanks, I will." She paused for a second, then put on the coat and said,

"You're not so bad, Jenny. I'm sorry I've been so unfriendly to you all this time, but my mother won't let me be friendly with, what she calls, skating rivals. She actually frightens me with her determination."

"That's okay. I figured it was something like that." replied Jenny.

A few minutes later Jenny went back into the dressing room, and Fiona got up and walked around. It couldn't have been made any easier for the new kidnappers because Fiona was walking near the goods entrance just as they came in.

"That must be her. Look at the coat." said one of the kidnappers.

"Excuse me, Miss." said the first kidnapper, holding up a piece of paper. "Do you know where this is in the arena?"

Fiona came over to them to read it. The kidnappers had a quick look around them and then, quick as lightning, grabbed her and held a wad of cloth over her mouth and nose. She struggled for a few seconds, but then passed out. They quickly picked her up and carried her out to their van, where they bundled her into the back and drove off.

Meanwhile, Helen was beginning to get nervous, and paced up and down for about ten minutes. Then, she went down to the dressing rooms to find Fiona.

"Charles. Where's Fiona? Aren't you supposed to be supervising her warm up?"

"Yes, I am, but I haven't seen her around. I thought she was with you, and I'm getting a bit worried because she needs to start warming up now."

Helen looked into every dressing room, but couldn't find her daughter. She started to panic.

"Where is security? Call security!"

A few moments later, security officers arrived and asked what was the matter.

"My daughter is nowhere to be found, and she's competing in about forty-five minutes. You have to find her." said Helen, becoming more and more distressed.

Jenny came out of the dressing room to see what all the fuss was about.

"Jenny!" said an anxious Helen. "Where's Fiona?"

"I don't know." replied Jenny, shrugging her shoulders. "The last time I saw her she was sitting on this bench, shivering like crazy, so I gave her my coat so that she could get warm."

"You WHAT?" said Helen, raising her voice. "No! NO! Why did you do that?"

"I just told you, Mrs. Forbes-Cunningham. So that she could get warm."

The realization of what had happened slowly came home to Helen. She looked completely shattered, and slumped down on the bench.

"Oh my God. Oh my God..." she kept repeating.

People started gathering around her, wondering why she was so distressed. Then, one of the competition officials came along to check if all the skaters were present. When he called out Fiona's name there was, obviously, no answer. He called out again.

"Is Fiona Forbes-Cunningham here? Has anyone seen her?"

No-one answered. Then, Helen got to her feet and went over to the official. She composed herself and then said,

"I'm her mother, and she won't be skating in this event."

Surprised, the official asked,

"Are you sure? Because we'll have to announce her withdrawal very soon, and the competition organizers will need time to re-arrange the skating order."

"Yes. I'm afraid I'm quite sure."

The official thanked her, and walked away.

Even in her shocked state, Helen had the presence of mind to go into the locker room and collect together all of Fiona's things. When she came out she sat down again on the bench and, by the look on her face, was trying to comprehend what had happened in the last couple of hours.

She was still trying to make sense of it several minutes later when an announcement came over the loudspeakers.

"We have to announce that Fiona Forbes-Cunningham is a late withdrawal from the Ladies Championship here today."

You could hear the gasps from around the stadium. I rushed over to where Helen was sitting.

"Helen! What's happened? Where is Fiona?"

"I don't know, Charles. I really don't know. Maybe she couldn't take the pressure, and has run away."

"Well try not to worry, Helen. We'll find her, and everything will be alright. You'll see." I said, trying to console her as much as I could.

I collared one of the officials and explained as much as I could.

"I think you'd better call the police right away. Something's happened to Fiona, and her mother, here, is at her wits end."

"We'll do that right now, Mr. Williams." he replied, reaching for his intercom.

I could hear him calling the competition organizers, telling them that the police needed to be called immediately. After a few minutes, they got back to him.

"Mrs. Forbes-Cunningham. The police would like you to stay right here until they arrive."

"Alright." she replied.

"Will you be alright for a few minutes, Helen? I have to get Jenny warmed up."

"Yes, you go right ahead, Charles." she replied, staring into the distance. She looked totally shattered.

I went and found Jenny and started going through her usual warm-up routine.

"Oh, Mr. Williams," said Jenny, wincing. "I can hardly move some parts of my body. I'm never going to be able to get through my program."

"You can do it, Jenny. You can get yourself ready. Think what this means to you. All the hours of training and sacrifice, your mum and dad's hopes for you, your own personal dreams?"

She thought for a moment, and then a look of determination came over her face.

"Yes...I think I can. I read in school once about a mighty warrior who had been beaten and badly injured, but he knew the only hope to save his village was to defeat his mortal enemy, and so he drew on every ounce of strength he had to prepare himself for one final battle. He thought about how proud his ancestors would be of him if he could fight through the pain and emerge triumphant. And he did. So, if he could do it, I can do it"

"Well there you are Jenny. Now you have your own private battle to win...and you will."

As Jenny continued to warm up and do all her stretching exercises, I could see her fighting back the tears as she tried to overcome the pain. Who couldn't admire someone so determined. If anyone ever deserved to win a championship, it was her.

"Put on a little extra make-up, Jenny. Then you'll look even better than Miss Australia."

Jenny smiled, and nodded.

In the past, when I competed, I'd had some very apprehensive moments in the hour or so before a competition, but what I felt then was nothing compared to how I was feeling now. I felt helpless, and it was a horrible feeling. All these months of her training, and of my hopes for her, could so easily go right out the window. I didn't want to keep fussing around her, but, as her coach, I wanted to make sure I'd said all that I needed to say.

"Okay, Jenny, let's go through your program to the music."

I set up my boom box and pushed the button.

Jenny went through her program making sure that she was doing exactly the right thing on each musical indication. Many of her jumps and spins were choreographed to be where the music reached a crescendo, so she had to know exactly when to take off, or go into a spin, in order to be in sync with the music score. When the body does what the music suggests, it makes for a greater impact on the judges and audience.

"You'd better get your skates on now, Jenny. It won't be long before your warm up."

"Okay, Mr. Williams. Will do."

Just then, one of the officials came around to make sure that all the skaters would be ready for their warm up.

"Okay, girls, the warm up for the second group will be in about twenty minutes, so don't be late."

I'm sure the gladiators in Roman times felt the same as we did as we walked through the tunnel into the arena. The feeling of anxiety as you sense the expectations of the crowd. The only difference being that half the gladiators knew they would probably be leaving the arena on a stretcher which, fortunately, wasn't going to be the case in our upcoming event. Thank goodness *our* audience wouldn't be looking for such a blood-curdling ending to the proceedings.

For many skaters, standing around waiting to go onto the ice for their warm up is the worst part. You just want to get out there and get on with it. But, we didn't have to wait too long.

"Will the next group of skaters take the ice for their warm up." said the announcer.

The girls took to the ice and you could feel the audience's excitement. As each skater's name was announced there would be cheering from various parts of the arena, but none as loud as there was for Jenny. I hoped that she was concentrating on the job in hand, because the cheering could distract her.

I really didn't have to say much to Jenny because she knew exactly what to do, and the warm-up went very well.

Well, this was it. All the months of training had come down to this moment, and now it seemed like the time had gone by so quickly. It didn't seem that long ago that I first met Jenny and her parents, and in a relatively short space of time that rough diamond had grown up into a polished gem.

"How do you feel, Jenny?" I asked.

"Really stiff and sore, to tell the truth. But I'm going to go for it."

"I know you will, Jenny. We're all so proud of you. Here, have a sip of water. You'll be on in a couple of minutes."

Those couple of minutes went by quickly, and I had one final thing to say to her as she stepped onto the ice.

"Whatever you manage to do, Jenny, will be fine. You're the best."

She looked at me, and cracked a little smile, knowing that it was all up to her, now.

"And now, ladies and gentlemen," the announcer called out. "Please welcome our next skater. Representing the Skating Club of Warragong Springs...Jenny Atkins!"

She skated out to a tremendous reception, which must have made her heart feel good if nothing else, but when the applause died down you could feel the tension in the air.

"Oh, dear God," I thought. "Do whatever you like with *me*, but please see Jenny through this one...*please!*"

My heart was pounding, and then her music started playing. She moved off with great energy and started gaining speed for her first jump, a triple-double combination. She tapped into the ice and sprang up into the air. Triple Lutz...yes...and double loop...yes! Wow! How did she do that? That didn't all come from my coaching. This was followed by some nice artistic connecting moves into her next jump, a double axel. I hoped she remembered her take-off position and timing. She did!

She had begun nicely, and I was sure that it was the adrenaline coursing through her veins that was acting as a pain-killer. And she must have been sensing by now that she could make it through to the end. As she skated fairly close by me on her way to the next jump, she managed to give me a quick look, as if to reassure me. What presence of mind!

After another successful triple jump, the next element was a combination spin with changes of position on both feet. I was glad I wasn't her. I knew she was going to have to contort her body into positions that were bound to hurt after her ordeal with the kidnappers. Jumping only required her body to be quite straight and just rotate, but these spin positions required her to twist her body into positions not unlike those she experienced when she was tied up in that shed.

She skated a nice strong edge into a camel spin to start the combination, but I could see the anguish on her face, knowing that she had to transition into a very low sit spin position. She brought her free leg around in front of her and got down as low as she could. I could see her wincing with pain, and then it was time to change onto her other foot for the second part of the combination, a back sit spin. This she managed to do fairly well, and then back to an upright position, grabbing her free leg behind her for a beautiful Biellmann spin. Her eyes were filled with tears, but she fought like a tiger to complete the element.

Right from the start of her program Jenny had put on a brave face, so the judges may not have realized what she was fighting through, but I knew this girl well, and I could see the pain, and determination, on her face. Every time she landed a jump she grimaced from the pain, but strived to hold herself together as she got closer to the end of the program. When she knew she was into the final minute she summoned up all her strength to pull off her remaining triple jump, and her final spin.

The audience, most of whom must have heard about her kidnapping, rose to their feet even before she'd finished the spin, and gave her a huge standing ovation.

Taking her final bow, she was a spent force and collapsed down onto her knees, but, being the girl she is, managed to get up again and skate off to the exit. I couldn't believe she'd pulled off this performance, but she had. She came off the ice weeping, and collapsed into my arms. I didn't realize it, but tears were running down my cheeks, too.

"Oh, my God, Jenny. You're a miracle on skates! What a performance!"

Jenny took a minute or two to recover, and then turned and waved to the audience. A new burst of applause erupted, and that brought a smile to her tired-looking face.

"Your mum must have gone through a whole box of Kleenex." I said. "Come on over here. They call this the 'Kiss and Cry' area, and you've done the crying, so I'll provide the kiss."

We sat down and, shortly after that, the marks came up.

"Wow, Jenny, these marks are going to be hard to beat, so let's keep our fingers crossed."

There were seven more girls to skate so we found a couple of seats to watch their performances.

"You know what, Mr. Williams? It would be nice to get a medal, but I don't care where I finish in the results, because forty-eight hours ago I could never have dreamed I'd even be here, let alone skate well."

"Yes, Jenny." I replied. "You've had quite a ride these last forty-eight hours."

We watched the remaining competitors perform their programs and then went back to the dressing room area to await the results.

It seemed an age before the results were made known. An official came down to the dressing room area and told three of the girls that they would be on the podium, but he wouldn't say in which order. And Jenny was one of them!

"We want to keep everything a surprise right up the last minute." he announced.

The ice was cleared and the podium was taken out to center ice.

"Okay, girls. Come and stand by the side of the ice, please." said the official.

In a bold, clear voice the announcer proclaimed,

"Ladies and gentlemen, I think you'll agree it's been a wonderful event, and I'm now going to announce the three medalists in reverse order."

After he had called out the names of the third and second placed girls he paused for a moment, and then said,

"And now, ladies and gentlemen, we have a new Australian Senior Ladies champion, and her name is...Jennifer Atkins!"

Once again, the audience erupted into a huge burst of applause, and people were yelling all sorts of compliments to Jenny, including three proposals of marriage! I know Bob and Lucy must have been trembling with excitement. I was told afterwards that Lucy *almost* feinted again.

Downstairs, Helen was still sitting on the bench by the dressing rooms. It's hard to know if she actually heard Jenny being announced as the new champion, or whether she was totally oblivious to anything going on around her. She looked so numb, I think it was the latter. It's also probable that Helen hadn't even begun to think about what the consequences would be if she were found out, which, eventually, she almost certainly would be. The evil that had manifested itself within her, and grown to almost consume her, had eventually become her undoing.

Almost certainly, she loved her daughter so much that she would do almost anything to bring her success, but, of course, some people go too far. Yes, on the face of it, she was a bad person, but even a stopped clock is right twice a day.

"Mrs. Forbes-Cunningham?"

"Yes?"

"We're police officers. We've come to tell you that a kidnap attempt was made on your daughter, but it was foiled by one of our officers in a patrol car about twenty miles out of town. He saw a speeding van and made the driver stop. When the officer got out of his car he heard a muffled cry from inside the van and investigated. It was your daughter, so all I can say, Mrs. Forbes-Cunningham, is that you must be feeling that you're a very lucky woman. You must be overjoyed that the kidnappers were foiled."

Helen, looking completely drained, physically and mentally, replied, "Oh...yes."

"Are you alright, Mrs. Forbes-Cunningham? I know this must be a big shock to you." said the officer. "But it just shows how evil, and desperate, some people can be."

"Yes...thank you officer." replied Helen. "Where is my daughter, now?"

"She's at the police station, where they're looking after her. She's in quite a state of shock, and appears to be dumbstruck. I'm sure she needs you."

"Alright. If you would be so kind as to write down the name and address of the Police station, I'll be along soon to pick her up."

"Well, it's not quite as simple as that, ma'am. The Federal Police are going to need to question her, but it would be best if you were there."

Helen sat there for a while and then got up. Wheeling the case behind her, she quietly left the arena. She would almost certainly be facing criminal charges in the not-too-distant future, but her self-inflicted punishment had already started. She now had to live with herself. And she realized that once the new kidnappers were questioned they would very likely reveal everything they knew in order to get a lighter prison sentence, and that it was only going to be a matter of time before the authorities caught up with her. Once the evidence was weighed up it would prove, overwhelmingly, that it was she who masterminded the kidnappings.

On the ice the award ceremony was under way. The three ladies were standing on the podium with their medals around their necks, each holding a bouquet of flowers in their arms. The audience gave them a well-deserved ovation, and I heaved a sigh of relief. All the hard work, the dramas, the setbacks, and the hundred other things that can get in the way, all boiled down to this moment.

I looked across the ice at the podium and took a photograph in my mind of Jenny standing there. A picture I could keep forever.

Once the girls got off the podium they skated a lap of honour, waving to the crowd. Then, it was skates off, a short press conference, and a host of friends, family and relatives swarming all over the place taking photographs and congratulating the skaters. It's always a bit chaotic and overwhelming after a championship, but eventually life would return to normal.

19

By Monday morning all the excitement had died down, and life was definitely getting back to normal.

While they were having breakfast, Lucy reminded Jenny that she wouldn't be going to school until the afternoon.

"Jenny, you remember I told you that we have a Superintendent from the Federal Police coming this morning to talk with you about the incident, but I don't know how long it's going to take."

"Yes, I remember, mum. I hope he's nice."

"Oh, I'm sure he will be. You just answer all his questions and I'm sure he'll be happy."

About twenty minutes later a car drew up outside their house, and two men got out. They walked up to the front door and rang the bell. Lucy opened the door.

"Mrs. Atkins? I'm Superintendent Miller from the Federal Police department, and this is Sergeant Mayhew. May we come in?"

"Oh, yes. Please do. Bob, Jenny, this is Superintendent Miller and Sergeant Mayhew from the Federal Police."

"I'm pleased to meet you, sir." said Bob. "And thank you so much for coming."

Lucy took their coats, and ushered them into the living room.

"Please sit down and be comfortable, and I'll make some tea."

"That'd be very nice, Mrs. Atkins. Our throats *are* a bit dusty after our long drive."

The tea arrived, and was, apparently, very welcome.

"That was lovely, Mrs. Atkins. Just hit the spot. But now, I'm afraid, we have to get down to business, so I know this is not going to be easy, Jenny, but try to tell us exactly what happened. Sergeant Mayhew will take notes."

"Okay, sir, I'll try."

Jenny then related the whole frightening experience in such detail that she broke down occasionally, and had to take a minute or two to wipe away the tears.

The Superintendent gave her time to recover, and then explained,

"Alright, Jenny. You've been a brave girl, and I'm sorry I had to make you re-live it all again, but this will help us enormously.

First of all, I want you and your parents to know that we, the Australian Federal Police, automatically put out an all points bulletin to all airports, sea ports, and railway stations in cases like this, in the hope that the perpetrators haven't already left the country.

Now, this is a fairly complicated situation, which, of course, will be made a lot simpler if we can apprehend the three of them. Even one of them would be enough. Then, as the evidence against them is so overwhelming, the chances are they'll confess to the crime and make a deal for a lighter sentence by telling us who paid them to do it. Now, Jenny, you said that when you were held captive in the shed you heard them say they were going to collect the money, and when they got back they were in a very good mood, so the chances are, they got it?"

"Yes." replied Jenny. "They brought a crate of beer back with them to celebrate, so I know they must have collected the money."

"Right, Jenny. But, Bob and Lucy, here's where it gets difficult. We're pretty sure they were paid a large sum, especially as you say that Alice said they were all leaving the country to start a new life, and a new life doesn't come cheap. So the way I see it is this. They could have bought another vehicle and be heading in any direction in this huge country of ours, they could have paid the skipper of a small boat to be waiting for them anywhere along the coast, or even a pilot of a small plane. They could buy new clothes, and even a new identity, so it's not going to be easy catching them, but we'll do it."

Bob and Lucy looked quite concerned.

"Do you really think so, Superintendent?" said Lucy. "It's frightening to think that this could happen to any child out there."

"Yes, I understand what you're saying, but this was a one-off situation almost certainly motivated by the maniacal actions of a very desperate person. It looks very much like Helen Forbes-Cunningham was behind it, but, so far, we have absolutely no conclusive evidence whatsoever to prove it. And I think it's fair to say that there hasn't been a kidnapping in this area before now, and probably won't be in the future."

"Well, we haven't been living here very long, so I wouldn't know, but I'm sure you're right." replied Lucy.

"So," the Superintendent went on, "We'll be keeping in touch with you, probably every day, letting you know how things are progressing."

"Thank you, Superintendent." said Lucy. "In a way, though, this kind of makes me lose faith in mankind because, although we've always told Jenny never to get into a car with a strange man, this is someone she knew, so I don't know what to say."

"Well, I guess it means you can never be too careful."

"No, that's true." said Bob.

"Now, let me tell you about what happened at the arena. Under questioning, the two men who kidnapped Fiona said everything was arranged so quickly they never knew who was behind it, and that they were going to be paid afterwards. We believe them because they would get a much lighter sentence if they'd come up with a name. But they did say that a man called Chris put them up to the kidnapping, so if we do catch him he'll be on two kidnapping charges.

So, thank you for meeting with me. I'd better get back to the office, now, and see how the investigation is going."

As the Superintendent drove away Jenny and her parents waved goodbye until his car was a speck in the distance.

20

On a Brighter Note

⁓ ◡ ⁓

Not for the first time, there was an urgent phone call to the Atkins' household.

"Lucy!" said an excited Ralph Johnson. "Can you, Bob, and Jenny come down to the rink this afternoon? The Mayor of Warragong Springs has a surprise presentation to make to Jenny."

"Why, yes, certainly." replied Lucy. "About what time?"

"Right after school would be ideal."

"Okay, thanks Ralph. We'll be there."

Later that day, skaters and parents gathered in the lobby of the ice rink in readiness for the arrival of the Mayor. A table had been set out for him and the Lady Mayoress.

"Ooh, this is quite exciting, but I do feel nervous." said Jenny.

Just then a car drew up outside and out stepped the Mayor, carrying a large diploma. Everyone applauded as he stepped into the rink.

"Welcome to our humble ice rink." said Ralph Johnson, greeting the honored guests. "It's not very official-looking, but we've set up a table for you stand behind."

"That will be fine, Ralph." replied the Mayor, taking up his position.

"Ladies and gentlemen, The last thing I want to do is bore you with a long-winded speech, so I'm going to keep this informal, and nice and short. Jenny Atkins, would you step forward, please?"

Jenny stepped forward, looking more nervous than I'd ever seen her.

The Mayor then held up a very official-looking diploma and shook Jenny's hand.

"In recognition of your magnificent achievement of winning the National Ice Skating Championship, I award you the freedom of the city...even though it's only officially a town!" Then he added.

"But that doesn't allow you to climb the trees in the main street!" That made everyone laugh.

"Oh, wow, that's great!" beamed Jenny. "And I probably shouldn't say this, but I always felt like I could do anything I wanted in Warragong Springs, anyway."

Now, it was the Mayors turn to laugh.

After the formalities, the mayor and his wife mingled with the parents and skaters, and enjoyed a few informal moments before leaving. When they did, everyone gave them an appreciative round of applause.

After the mayor had left, Lucy realized that most of her friends were there, so she called out,

"Listen, everyone, I want you all to come to a celebration dinner at our place this Saturday. As we don't know how many will be coming, we'll have a buffet-style dinner and you can grab a chair if you can find one, or better still, bring your own."

One of the other parents spoke up.

"Lucy. There'll be so many people who will want to come to the celebration, it's going to cost you a fortune in food, so I'm sure we'd all be only too pleased to each bring a plate of food and some other things. That way, they'll be a big variety of dishes and plenty to go around.

"Oh, Barbara, that's a lovely idea. Thank you so much."

"You're welcome, Lucy. So it's all set, then. I'll spread the word, and I think we'll definitely bring some extra chairs, too."

Saturday came, and there was great excitement at the Atkins' house. Lucy had been house cleaning all week, and was now setting out tables inside and outside the house, complete with colorful floral arrangements placed on them. She had also put a big picture of Jenny, receiving her gold medal, on the wall, surrounded by ribbons and lots of golden hearts.

The first guests started to arrive around five p.m. The women went straight to Lucy and started chatting, the men went straight to the refrigerator for a cold beer. Every few minutes a few more people would arrive, and follow the same pattern. The house was starting to buzz with excitement. It seemed like everyone in Warragong Springs was going to be there. 'Speedy', 'Brains', 'Munchy', and other skaters and their parents turned up soon after, followed by Billy Cameron, Ralph Johnson, and the entire ice rink staff. Soon, the party was in full swing. There was food and drink everywhere, and everyone was enjoying themselves. Luckily, someone was standing near the telephone.

"Lucy." someone called out. "The phone's ringing."

Lucy went over and picked it up. She listened for a few seconds and then shouted out,

"Charlie, it's your mother, calling from England."

"Oh, my God!" I exclaimed. "Don't tell me something's happened to dad." Then I said to myself, "Please God, no bad news."

Lucy handed me the phone.

"Mum? What's happened? Is dad okay?"

My mother quickly replied,

"Yes, of course he is. He's never been better."

I butted in before she could continue,

"Oh, thank God for that. I thought something had happened to him, and that was why you were calling, but it's great to hear your voice, mum. It must cost a lot to call from England, so what is it? Is everything alright?"

"Yes. And if you'll just close your mouth for a minute or two and let me explain, we've got some amazing news for you."

"Okay. What is it?"

"It's literally front page news. It's Sunday morning, here, and when dad picked up the newspaper this morning and read it, he nearly fell over backwards. There on the front page was a headline, 'Champion ice skater confesses', and then underneath it said, 'Jimmy Donovan tells all'. He's come clean, Charlie, and admitted that he lied about you giving him drugs."

My mouth dropped open, and I couldn't believe my ears. Mum continued,

"I'll read out what it says.

'In a surprisingly frank admission, the Junior Men's National ice skating champion has come forward to confess that he lied to the Skating association and the press about his coach giving him drugs. He also went on to say that his conscience had been tormenting him, and now that he's had plenty of time to think about it, he realizes the terrible thing he's done, and can't go on living a lie. He said he took the performance enhancing drug because he was desperate to skate well in his first international event, and needed to do everything possible to avoid losing, because that would almost certainly result in a beating from his father, a man who could not tolerate failure.'"

"Wow, mum, this is such a relief. Everyone will know now that I'm innocent."

"Well, there's a bit more, Charlie, and he mentions you at the end. I'll read the rest.

'He went on to say that he always lived in fear of his father's reaction whenever he skated badly, but now says that he eventually faced up to him, and will take the consequences. It's common knowledge that his father was sent to prison for four years, but there will also be a restraining order on him forbidding him to go anywhere near his son when he comes out.

He also said that he just hoped that Charlie Williams, the coach who was banned from teaching in Great Britain because of his lies, and whose reputation was ruined by this affair, can one day forgive him.'"

"So you see, Charlie, I called because we wanted to let you know immediately. A letter would have taken too much time to get there."

"Oh, mum, I can't thank you enough. And I know it's an old cliché, but, obviously, I really feel like a huge weight has been lifted off me.

This is fantastic, and I feel like I'm re-born. Just a second, mum, while I quickly tell everyone here."

I turned around and yelled out,

"Hey, everyone, this is my mother calling from England, and she's just told me that the boy who made the accusation about me has admitted he lied. I'm proven completely innocent."

Everyone in the room cheered and congratulated me on the good news.

"So this is a double celebration here this evening. Thanks, everyone!"

I got back on the phone with my mother and told her how happy everyone was here. She said I didn't need to tell her because she could here all the excitement in the background.

"Oh, Charlie," his mother continued, "Our phone hasn't stopped ringing all morning. Just about everyone who knows you, and some that don't, have called to say how happy they are for you. But the call that I know you'll be happiest about was from Miss Cook. She sounded positively excited!"

"Wonderful!" I replied. "That means so much to me. And this is the perfect time for me to fly back to England. The championships are over, and I could do with a little break. I can even use the return portion of my frequent flyer ticket, so I'll let you know as soon as I've booked the flight."

I heard mum heave a huge sigh of relief.

"Oh, it'll be so nice to have you home again, even if it may not be for long."

21

A SHORT TRIP BACK TO ENGLAND

After flying half way around the world again, the plane touched down at Heathrow. And I must admit, although it felt so good to be back in England, I should have realized that some things never change.

I hadn't walked ten paces out of baggage claim when I was confronted with the same group of press boys that had been happy to see the back of me several months ago. And yet, here they were again, virtually welcoming me back. It was like running the movie backwards.

"Sorry, Charlie. I guess we gave you a hard time last time we saw you."

"Well, you boys always jump to conclusions, don't you? It's the only exercise you get."

"I suppose we deserve that." said another journalist. "But we really are glad that you've been proven innocent. No hard feelings?"

"No. No feelings at all, really. I just want life to get back to normal."

As soon as the press boys had dispersed I saw the best sight I could wish for. My whole family.

"Oh, my God." I exclaimed. You're all here!"

"We wanted to give you the best welcome home a person could get, and we couldn't think of a better way." said my mother. "So let's get home now and have a real celebration!"

That evening, just about everyone I knew managed to squeeze themselves into our house. And it was not a big house. There was an even mix of jubilation and relief in the air, and it was great to see each person in turn.

"Miss Cook!" I exclaimed. "This is such an honor having you here in our house. I can't believe it."

"Well, believe it, because I wouldn't have missed this for the world. I'm as relieved about this matter as you are, Charlie. It's wonderful."

And she gave me an unexpected, huge hug.

After an hour or so I thought I'd seen everyone, but then a figure emerged from the crowd and came towards me.

"Jimmy!" I gasped. "I didn't think you'd be here, but I'm glad you are."

"Charlie. Can you *ever* forgive me? I'm actually afraid to talk to you."

"Don't be, Jimmy. At first, it *was* the end of my world, but you know what they say, 'The Lord works in mysterious ways, his wonders to perform', and, eventually, things worked out fairly well. In fact, I really don't know how things would have turned out if I'd stayed here, so there you are."

"Thanks, Charlie. You're making me feel better already."

"Well, Jimmy, when the facts came out, everyone, including myself, understood your predicament, but now your life, too, is probably going to start taking a turn for the better, very soon. You'll be competing again in a few months, and under a lot less pressure, I'm sure, but stay with Arthur Begley, and I wish you the very best of luck."

Just about the last person I got around to seeing was my old skating pal, Don.

"Charlie, old buddy! It really is great to see you. We all knew the truth would come out in the end, but that it would take a little while.

We've been following your fortunes in Australia, and you're obviously a big hit over there. Do you think you'll stay there?"

"I really don't know, Don. I'm just going to play it by ear and see how things turn out. But I'm leading a very happy life 'down under'. How are things going with you?"

"Well, guess what? Louise and I are getting engaged."

"Oh, my goodness. Congratulations, Don!"

"Thanks, Charlie. And, of course, that means that Cathy is still available."

"What are you? The local matchmaker? Anyway, there is someone I'm hoping might come back to me when she learns the truth about what happened, so I'll leave Cathy out of the equation right now. But thanks."

Over the next couple of days phone calls came in from everywhere, including some parts of Europe where I'd asked to teach, but where I was flatly turned down. Now, it was a case of, "Oh, we would love you to come and teach here, Charlie." Well, thank you very much, but keep your job offer.

Each morning I was home my mother brought me a cup of tea in bed. She always thought that was a nice way to start the day.

"Here you are, Charlie. I like to spoil you while you're home."

"Thanks, mum. I don't get this treatment in Australia."

I took a few sips and then said,

"I think I'd better book my flight to go back soon. And then I'll have some real thinking to do now that I know I can teach anywhere I want."

"Well." mum replied. "Take your time, because you want to do the right thing, and it's nice that you're now spoiled for choice. And another thing, Charlie, dad's retiring soon, with a nice pension, so if you do want to live in Australia we could always spend a few weeks with you every year. It's just a thought."

"No, mum. That's a good thought."

I finished my tea, and then got up to shave and shower. I had several things to attend to, and I would be out all day long.

That evening, at dinner, the atmosphere was certainly a whole lot nicer than it was the night before I went to Australia for the first time.

"I booked my flight, so I'll be leaving the day after tomorrow, dad."

"Okay, son. I'll make sure I get the time off to take you to the airport."

As usual, the time went by quickly, and before I knew it I was on my way to Heathrow Airport yet again.

"You know, mum and dad, even if I don't stay in Warragong Springs, I'd love you to come and meet all the people there. It's like being part of a huge family, and everyone looks after everyone else, and nearly everyone smiles."

22

JENNY REPRESENTS AUSTRALIA

I was enjoying a long sleep to get over my jetlag from the flight back to Australia when I heard a familiar voice. It was Billy.

"Charlie? Are you in your room?"

"Yes. What's up?" I replied.

"Come down and pick up the phone. It's Lucy."

I rushed downstairs, hoping that nothing was wrong.

"Hi, Lucy. What is it?"

"Guess what, Charlie? The association just called, and they want Jenny to go to an international event."

"That's great! Which one is it?"

"Budapest."

"Oh my God! This takes my life full circle." I replied, smiling to myself. "When is it?"

"It's in about six weeks time, so they said she'll have plenty of time to prepare for it, and get a passport and so on."

"Wow. This *is* exciting. And we have plenty of time to plan everything well. Can I invite myself over to dinner tonight? Then I can fill you in on a lot of the details."

"Of course, Charlie. We'll look forward to seeing you, around seven."

"Thank you. I'll be there for sure."

That evening, Lucy greeted me at the door.

"Welcome back, Charlie. I hope you had a great time in England."

"Yes, I did, thanks Lucy. It was great, in so many ways."

"Oh, I am pleased. And, apart from Jenny being selected for the international event, a lot of other things have been happening since you went away. Superintendent Miller of the Federal Police Dept. called to say that they had apprehended Chris, John and Alice Carson. They had obtained fake passports and were about to board a plane for Singapore, when an official recognized one of them from a police photograph.

Now, as for Helen, there is overwhelming evidence that she masterminded the kidnappings, and Chris Carson and his siblings are going to testify that Helen paid them. That way, they'll get shorter prison sentences. Helen, however, has disappeared from the face of the earth. She was probably clever enough to have an escape plan, should the kidnapping go wrong, but even if they never catch her she'll be facing the prospect of never seeing Fiona again if she wants to avoid capture. And I can tell you, from a mother's point of view, that would be like going through a living hell if, as I suspect, she really did love her daughter.

Fiona, bless her, is now in the custody of her father, but I really don't know what her plans are."

Over dinner, I explained about international events, and what to expect.

"First of all, it makes you feel very proud to represent your country, and you often get to go to a really nice place where you can do some sightseeing, buy some souvenirs, and make new friends. And although it sounds very grand going to an 'international event', there's often less pressure on you to skate well there than there would be at some of your home events. I used to say to myself that if I messed up it wasn't the end of the world because I probably wouldn't see these people again, anyway, unlike at home. And then there's the food. It might be a bit different to what you're used to, but they usually try to cater to everyone."

"It sounds wonderful, Charlie." said Lucy. "I'm going got be able to go with Jenny, but Bob's staying here. Someone's got to keep the home fires burning."

"Well, we'll take lots of photographs to show Bob what it was all about." I said.

I made Jenny take a few days off to get her mind completely off ice skating, so that when she returned to training she would have a steady five-week buildup in preparation for the event.

A few days later, word got around the rink that Fiona had decided to take advantage of the offer she was made to join the Australian Ballet.

"Oh, my God." said Jenny, looking very sad. "I'll miss her. If anything, she pushed me to become a better skater, but I know she'll be happy there."

"Yes." I replied. "And although she had nothing to do with all the trouble, I think she might have found it embarrassing coming back into the ice rink."

"Well." Jenny added. "I'm going to write to her, and ask her to tell us when she's going to perform. I think it would be great to go and see her."

"Yes, that's a nice idea, Jenny. And I'm sure your mum and dad would like that, too."

During the five weeks leading up to our departure, Jenny became stronger and more artistic, and gained an even higher level of confidence. She was at the peak of her form, and Ralph Johnson arranged a wonderful send-off party at the rink.

"God bless you, Jenny, for a safe trip, and a great skate." he said, trying to be heard over the crowd. "We're mighty proud of you."

"Thanks, Mr. Johnson." replied Jenny. "I'll do my best."

After that, Lucy, Jenny, and I got in the car, and Bob drove us to Melbourne International Airport. We were on our way!

23

A Pleasant Surprise

~⁓◦◦⁓~

"Wow! That was a long flight." said a weary Jenny.

"Yes." replied Lucy. "I just want to get to the hotel and sleep for a while. Do you ever get used to this, Charlie?"

"Not really, Lucy. We're always a bit jet-lagged for the first couple of days. But that's why we've come here several days before the event."

Fortunately, the hotel beds were extremely comfortable, and we caught up on sleep in a big way.

The next day, it was time to get down to business.

At the accreditation desk the skaters were given a badge, some welcoming items, and a competition program. We quickly turned the pages to Jenny's event so that we could see her opposition. As I looked down the list one of the names sprang out at me. *CYNTHIA HOLMES.* Cindy! My heart skipped a beat as I wondered if she would even talk to me. The news of my innocence had got to all four corners of the skating world, and I just prayed that it had reached her, too, but I didn't think any more about it, because I figured we'd bump into each other sooner or later at the competition. I was there as an official coach, and had a responsibility to do the best I could for my skater, so I couldn't let personal matters interfere with my work.

Everyone was staying in the same hotel, and while we were having dinner we saw the United States team enter the dining room. Cindy spotted me immediately and walked over to our table.

"Hello, Charlie." she said, timidly.

"Hello, Cindy. I'd like you to meet Lucy and her daughter, Jenny, who, I'm proud to say, is the Australian ladies champion."

Cindy shook hands with them, and looked very pleased to meet them. Then she came over and sat down beside me.

"Charlie. I can't tell you how sorry I am that I was so hasty in my judgment of you over that horrible affair. I feel terrible, having believed what I read in the newspapers without knowing the real truth. I should have waited until I heard your side of the story. Please, please forgive me."

"Of course I do, Cindy. And I'm so glad you're here because we can talk face to face. When did you hear about it?"

"Oh, about five weeks ago. Someone showed me the sports section of their newspaper, and it had the story of how your skater finally owned up and told the truth. I was so relieved, and I wanted to contact you immediately, but I was too scared to because I thought you'd be angry with me. And I couldn't bear that."

"I could never be angry with you, Cindy, so let's find some time tomorrow to have a long chat. Now, you'd better go and join your team, otherwise there won't be any dinner left."

"Okay, Charlie." she replied, smiling happily. "See you tomorrow."

The next day, we did find some time to talk. And, boy, did we talk. It was such a relief to clear the air with Cindy, and fill her in on some of the smaller details.

"Oh, Charlie, I can't believe how deceitful Jimmy was."

"He had to be, Cindy. Otherwise he knew he would be facing another beating from his father. He was between a rock and a hard place, but, fortunately, his life should become a lot better, now."

"Well, let's hope so." Cindy replied. "Everything does seem to be moving in the right direction, now."

"And you're moving like a champion on the ice, Cindy. You should have a great chance of winning, and you know I genuinely wish you the best of luck. My girl's only just getting into the big league, so we're just hoping for a good skate, and the opportunity to gain more experience. So I'll see you tomorrow at the rink. Sleep well!"

"You, too, Charlie. Sleep well."

At the practice session the next day I bumped into almost all the people I used to know. Herr Schnabel, Mme. Laurisse, Senor Gambelli, Igor Malkov, and a few others. And guess what? They were *so* pleased to see me. My goodness, I thought, how people change.

"That was a very good practice, Jenny." I said, as she came off the ice.

"Yes. I felt quite good out there." she replied. "Except the ice felt different to how it is at home. It's much harder, here."

"That's because the temperature in our rink back home is much warmer, and the ice is a bit softer. But you're skating well on this ice."

"Yes, boss." she said, with a silly smile on her face. "I'm ready to give it my best shot."

We had one more day of practice before the day of the competition, and Jenny continued to skate well. That's the thing about most skaters who are on their way up. They skate freely, and without worry, because they're not so much in the public eye. It's only when they get to the top that they start to feel the tension because so much more is *expected* of them.

So, the big day arrived. Jenny was in the second warm-up group, and Cindy, the fourth. At least Jenny had completely recovered from her kidnapping ordeal, and felt no ill-effects. That's the thing about young bodies. They heal quickly.

"Okay, Jenny." I said. "I'm not going to give you any specific instructions. Just go out there and enjoy your performance."

"I will, Mr. Williams. You'll see."

And I did see. A lovely performance from a girl who really enjoyed her skating.

"Well done, Jenny! That was worth flying halfway around the world to see."

Lucy, almost in tears, came running down to ice level to congratulate her daughter, and we all had a big group hug.

After everyone had calmed down, Jenny took off her skates and then we stayed so that we could watch Cindy skate a bit later. And skate she did! She had improved tremendously over the past year, and was in a class of her own. The result was never in much doubt. Cindy won, but, to our great surprise, Jenny finished third. We were absolutely over the moon.

"That's wonderful, Jenny." I said. "But you have to realize, Cindy always wins in Budapest. It's in the rules!"

Once again, though, it was a joy to see Jenny on a podium. But this time, an international podium. That made it all the more special.

After the competition, we were all waiting for the bus to take us back to the hotel when a couple, with a little girl, walked up to me.

"Mr. Williams? Are you Mr. Williams?"

"Yes, I'm Charlie Williams."

"This is our daughter. You saved her life. We cannot thank you enough."

"Oh, my God! Then she's alright."

The little girl let go of her parent's hands and rushed up to me, flinging her arms around me.

"Oh, my God, I'm so pleased to see you." I said, kneeling down on the ground to give her a hug. And the tears just ran down my cheeks.

Her parents didn't understand very much English, but I tried to explain.

"At first, when I got back to England, it seemed like a tragedy - you know? Like a very bad thing. But after that, my life took many different directions, and then everything turned out well. Do you understand?"

"Yes." her father replied. "I understand what you are saying. We are very happy for you. And thank you, again."

After managing a little more conversation we shook hands, and their daughter gave me another hug. Then they left, waving to me frequently as they walked to the car park.

Shortly after that the bus arrived, and everyone started to board.

Cindy was standing with me as the last few people got on. Then, a voice called out,

"The bus is leaving soon."

"You know what, Charlie? said Cindy. "It's such a nice day. Why don't we walk back to the hotel?"

THE END

Printed in the United States
By Bookmasters